Naomi Stanley Kulp

# WAGON WHEELS
## &
# WILD ROSES

*Heirloom Recipes and Oregon Trail Stories*
*From the McCaw Family*
*1847 - 1995*

By
Naomi Stanley Kulp

Wild Rose Press, Federal Way, Washington

Copyright 1996 Naomi Stanley Kulp

Illustrations by Linda Newberry and Evelyn Hicks
Typeset in Adobe Garamond and New Baskerville

Printed in the U.S.A.
Second printing, April 1996

ISBN 0-9648782-0-8

Library of Congress Catalog Card Number 95-61820

Dedicated
To My Family

# Acknowledgments

Thank you to the McCaw cousins for sharing their old, treasured, family recipes, vignettes, and family histories from the Oregon Trail and to Maryly and Jim Dahlquist and Jennabelle McLean Vincent for sharing their McCaw family documents.

Special thanks to Kay and Dennis Stanley, Connie Shupe Plants, Mary Shupe McCarthy, Paul McCaw, Jane and Bill Williams, and Mae Jean and Gerald Williams for testing recipes; to Paul McCaw for writing the Introduction and several vignettes; to Roger Clark for editing assistance; and to Sharlene Nelson for encouragement and guidance.

Welcome professional advice and assistance have come from Lawrence L. Dodd, Archivist, and Lawrence Paynter, Instructional Media Services, at Whitman College, Walla Walla, Washington; Bill Burk, Director, Fort Walla Walla Museum; and Sieglinde Smith, Librarian, Research Library, Oregon Historical Society, Portland, Oregon.

# Contributors

| | |
|---|---|
| Dorothy Vernon Avril | Ruth & Robert H. McCaw |
| Alene Vernon Bedford | Sarita & Bill McCaw |
| Cristy Bergevin | Ruth McCaw Merrill |
| Kathleen McCaw Bergevin | Allie Kinder Neal |
| Maryly & Jim Dahlquist | Connie Shupe Plants |
| Lois McCaw Ellsaesser | Jerrianne Powell |
| Marilyn McCaw Griffin | Della Mae Erwin Sanders |
| Carolyn McCaw Houger | Patricia & John Sawyer |
| Steve D. Martin | Betty & Norman Stanley |
| Mary Shupe McCarthy | Kay & Dennis Stanley |
| Carmen and Bruce McCaw | Jennabelle McLean Vincent |
| Libby McCaw | Jane & Bill Williams |
| Paul McCaw | Mae Jean & Jerry Williams |

# Pioneers & Wild Roses

The pioneers were, in several ways, like the wild rose that grew beside the Oregon Trail. Sometimes called the Prairie Rose, it grew willingingly wherever its seed touched soil, putting down roots in new ground and adapting quickly to its new home. Tenacious and determined to survive, like the pioneers, it was a sturdy plant that could withstand hardship and thrive, putting out new shoots to bloom in the sunshine.

This wild rose was loved by all who discovered it growing along the Oregon Trail and who tucked their noses into its center to catch the sun-warmed fragrance. The flowers were often pressed in family Bibles as reminders that beauty is found in the most unexpected places.

After the wild rose bloomed in May and June, the clusters of rose hips would be bright red by late July and full of Vitamin C. Today it is believed that the pioneers ate the rose hips to prevent scurvy, probably gathering, drying, and storing them for use during the long journey west.

Many years ago wild roses rambled over the old post fence by the lane that led from our home down to the Touchet River. A few years ago I found the last little bush still growing in the same place, with blossoms as beautiful and fragrant as they were when I was a child. Now at home in my garden, it is thriving and a happy link to the past.

*Great grandparents William and Sarah Findley McCaw, 1880s.*

# Introduction

This collection of recipes, vignettes, and Oregon Trail family histories is a cameo of one pioneer family, the McCaws, that journeyed West by wagon train 148 years ago. We're proud of our unique heritage as descendents of those sturdy pioneers who followed their dream of a better life in the Willamette Valley, Oregon Territory and later in the Touchet Valley in Washington Territory. In the pages of this book we share our family recipes and memories with you. The book reflects the charm and happy times of growing up in our Touchet Valley and offers a glimpse into the kitchens of the past.

This book is primarily a cookbook. The recipes are tasty and nutritious, and some have endured for seven generations. Many were handed down from generation to generation in the McCaw family and are treasured for their usefulness and their link to our mothers and grandmothers.

The dishes we describe in the recipes are not fast food. Their preparation will take time, energy, and devotion. The ingredients are not exotic—they are the simple stuff of pioneers and farmers. But the results will reward those who take the time and energy to recreate them. A generation dependent on convenience foods will find it worthwhile to experience the fare of these folks who lived close to the soil, often close to danger and death.

This book has an additional purpose, however, because it is a history as well as a cookbook—the history of a pioneer family that came to the Pacific Northwest on the Oregon Trail. These were special people, who threw themselves into a wilderness with no more than a few rustic wagons and a spare few months' provisions. If there were any trail at all on the way to the Oregon Country, it was the faint trace of emigrations that had gone before. There were, along the trail, reminders of those who did not succeed.

We can learn by examining these lives—lives of immense courage as the pioneers battled against weather, topography, and Indian attacks. Optimism and a spirit of cooperation prevailed as they struggled to build a community in the wilderness. They were devoted to family and to the future of the fragile young community, as they quickly gave money from scarce resources to erect the Willamette Valley's first public building, a schoolhouse for their children, near Brownsville. Later, they went on to tame a different kind of wilderness and turn the fertile hills of Eastern Washington into one of the world's finest wheatlands.

Through it all, these hard-working people created their own relaxation and diversion and raised their children. They gathered large families together on special days to consume great tablesful of delicious food, made from the recipes contained in these pages.

The history embodied in this book goes to our roots, to a time when the vast majority of Americans were busy producing food. We like to think of these values as our best, referring to them as "family" or "traditional" values. When we despair over a nation that seems to have misplaced those values—of honesty, hard work, devotion to family, and self-respect—it is good for us to return to a time when they were as natural as the land this family loved and the food that it ate. This book allows us a window into that time.

*Paul McCaw*
*Old McCaw Farm*
*Prescott, Washington*

# Contents

## McCaw Family Recipes

## Oregon Trail Stories

*Children of Sarah and William McCaw and their spouses are: left to right, front row—Louisa Isobel McCaw, wife of Jeremiah Outman; Mary Jane McCaw Erwin; Samuel Erwin, husband of Mary; Geneva McNall McCaw, wife of John Newton McCaw. Middle row—Edwin Newman McCaw, Amanda Cordelia McCaw Erwin, David Erwin, husband of Amanda. Back row—Robert Cromwell McCaw; Ida Mae Murphy McCaw, wife of Edwin; Emmaline Gorsline, wife of Robert McCaw; John Newton McCaw.*

# Getting To Know
# The McCaw Family

### Oregon Trail Pioneers

In 1806 American explorers Lewis and Clark and their Indian guide Sacajawea, on their return from the Pacific Ocean, made their way up the valley of the Touchet River in southeastern Washington. In the early 1830s, after expedition leaders Wyeth and Bonneville led the way, a few hardy pioneers followed the general direction of the Lewis and Clark route, creating the Oregon Trail. One of the most famous of these pioneers was Marcus Whitman, who established a missionary outpost a few miles west of the modern city of Walla Walla, near the Washington and Oregon border in southeastern Washington.

### On the Trail to the Whitman Mission

In the early 1840s the federal government actively campaigned to encourage settlers to emigrate West to establish our country's claim on the Oregon Country.

Our great grandparents, William and Sarah McCaw, decided to join the thousands who were preparing for the long, difficult journey over the Oregon Trail. They departed Henderson County, Illinois with their oxen team and wagon on April 25, 1846. Their first destination was Independence, Missouri, a starting point for the Oregon Trail.

The small group encountered the usual problems. When driving their wagon through Lee County, Iowa, their daughter Mary Jane was born during the excitement of a buffalo stampede. They were delayed for some time making repairs and arrived in Independence too late to join a wagon train that year, forcing them to spend the winter there.

In the spring of 1847 they began their journey to Oregon Territory. On one occasion, when the wagon train was attacked by Indians, Mary Jane, then a toddler, was hidden in a small trunk until the attack was repelled. This trunk remains in the family. Mary Jane would eventually marry another pioneer, Sam Erwin, whose wagon train encountered a large Indian war party that wanted a particular member of their train. The man in question had sworn that he would kill an Indian before the expedition was over and finally shot an old woman who was gathering camas bulbs. Fearing for the safety of the entire train, the wagonmaster surrendered the young man, who suffered a swift retribution.

After enduring the long trek over the Oregon Trail, William and Sarah arrived at the Whitman mission in the fall. Dr. Marcus Whitman and his wife Narcissa had established their Presbyterian mission among the Indians at Waiilatpu. As part of the mission facility there was a blacksmith shop and a grist mill by the Walla Walla river for grinding flour and a lumber mill built by our cousin, Josiah Osborn, several miles into the nearby Blue Mountains. A branch of the Oregon Trail ran through the mission grounds; the wagon ruts are still visible today. The Whitmans offered shelter, food, medical help, and limited supplies to the weary travelers for their trip down the Columbia River to Oregon City.

## On to the Willamette Valley

Anxious to reach their final destination in the Willamette Valley, Oregon Territory, William and Sarah departed the mission with a small group in the middle of November. The wagon train followed the Columbia River downstream to The Dalles, where they stopped for a few days while the men whip-sawed lumber to build barges, rafts, and boats. Emigrants, wagons, and livestock were loaded for the trip downriver to Portland and then up the Willamette River to Oregon City. Many wagon trains chose the overland route and followed the Barlow Road around the southern slopes of Mt. Hood.

William McCaw, who earlier had lost his team of oxen and was forced to leave his wagon behind, was stricken at The Dalles with a fever so virulent he had to be carried on a stretcher for the remainder of the trip. He had to sell his cattle there to buy lumber to build rafts for the trip down the Columbia.

At Fort Vancouver, an outpost of the British Hudson's Bay Company located where the Willamette flows into the Columbia, Chief Factor Dr. John McLoughlin gave William credit. There, William bought a sack of beans—the main food his family had during their first hard winter in Oregon. Great grandfather always said it was more than enough beans to last a lifetime! William and Sarah arrived at Oregon City the day of the Whitman Massacre, November 29, 1847, and a few days later learned of this tragic event. A young cousin, Nancy Osborn, and her family, survived the Indian attack, hidden under the floorboards of the Whitman house.

*Opposite. 1901-1903. Family reunion at the home of Robert and Emmaline McCaw at Locust Lane. Back row (from left to right), Edwin McCaw, holding Dwight McCaw, Ida Murphy McCaw, Edith McCaw, Nellie Erwin, unknown, Louisa McCaw Outman, Mary McCaw Erwin, unknown, David Erwin, Amanda McCaw Erwin, unknown, Geneva McNall McCaw, unknown, unknown, Emmaline Gorsline McCaw, Robert C. McCaw holding Glen McCaw, John McCaw, and Elroy McCaw. Middle row. Mamie Outman, unknown, Will McCaw, Sam Erwin. Front row. Unknown, Sam McCaw, Fred McCaw, Guy McCaw, unknown, Harry McCaw, Marie McCaw, Ruth McCaw, Bessie McCaw, Jay McCaw, Margaret Erwin, Ethel McCaw, and Ada Erwin.*

*1991. McCaw family reunion in front of Samuel and Mary McCaw Erwin's stone home in Prescott.*

From Oregon City, their wagon train journeyed south about one hundred miles, following earlier wagon tracks. William and Sarah established their Donation Land Claim on Brush Creek near present day Crawfordsville and Brownsville. After many months of hardship on the Oregon Trail, they were thankful to build their homes in the Calapooia Valley near the foothills of the Cascade Mountains.

Virgin forests covered the Willamette Valley and grazing cattle were completely hidden in the tall grass. The mountains, with plentiful bear, beaver, cougar, deer, otter, elk, wildcat, and many smaller animals provided food and furs. Salmon and trout were caught in the streams and rivers. The homestead families also found abundant ducks and geese to grace their dinner tables and provide down and feathers for comforters and pillows.

William and Sarah found lots of good timber with which to build their log cabin. Friends helped them build and "plow round among the tree stumps." In the large garden they planted there, they grew beans, potatoes, pumpkins, squash, carrots, berries, and other fruits and vegetables. The wild Oregon Grape and salal provided berries for pies and jelly.

In the cabin's large fireplace, Sarah cooked for her growing family. On her beautiful spinning wheel, made for her by her cousin Josiah Osborn, she spun yarn. This spinning wheel is now at the Fort Walla Walla Museum in Walla Walla, Washington.

After the Oregon Territorial Bill was signed August 14, 1848, President Polk appointed Joseph Lane of Indiana territorial governor, and in 1849 Lane appointed our great grandfather to be Linn County clerk. Great grandfather was an important figure in establishing the early county government and later became one of the first county judges.

Determined to provide a school for their children, the thirteen local families gave small amounts of money (between $3 and $50), then built the frame schoolhouse 16 by 24 feet. William and Sarah's six children attended this school.

Life was often difficult in those early years and little money was available. Wheat was often used as the medium of exchange. Yet the families worked hard to build their community. Our great grandparents helped organize the Crawfordsville Presbyterian Church and were charter members. William was a ruling elder for fifteen years until they moved to Prescott, in Washington Territory, near Walla Walla. Prescott and Waitsburg, both important in our family history, are small towns eight miles apart on the Touchet River twenty miles north of Walla Walla. The snow-capped Blue Mountains rise at the eastern end of the fertile Touchet Valley. Touchet is an Indian word, pronounced Too-shee, that means "Salmon cooked over fire."

## From the Willamette to the Touchet Valley

William and Sarah's daughter Mary was nineteen when she married Sam Erwin. They were the first of our family to move (in 1860) to the Touchet Valley, where Sam had already established their farm and built their home. In the next few decades the other sons and daughters followed Sam and Mary, becoming owners of large wheat and cattle ranches in the Touchet Valley and surrounding area. Mary and Sam nurtured her brothers and sisters when they came to the valley, providing a home for them when needed and helping them establish their own farms. Of the entire family, Mary was the most loved. After 45 years in Crawfordsville, William and Sarah joined their children.

In the late 1800s Sam and Mary sold their farm and gave $6,000 to Whitworth College, at that time a small Presbyterian school in Tacoma, Washington. Later, the school named Erwin Hall for them. They were also charter members of the Presbyterian church in Waitsburg and worked hard for it.*

*Adapted from *Two Hundred Fifty Years of McCaws* by Robert H. McCaw, 1984.

# McCaw Family Tree

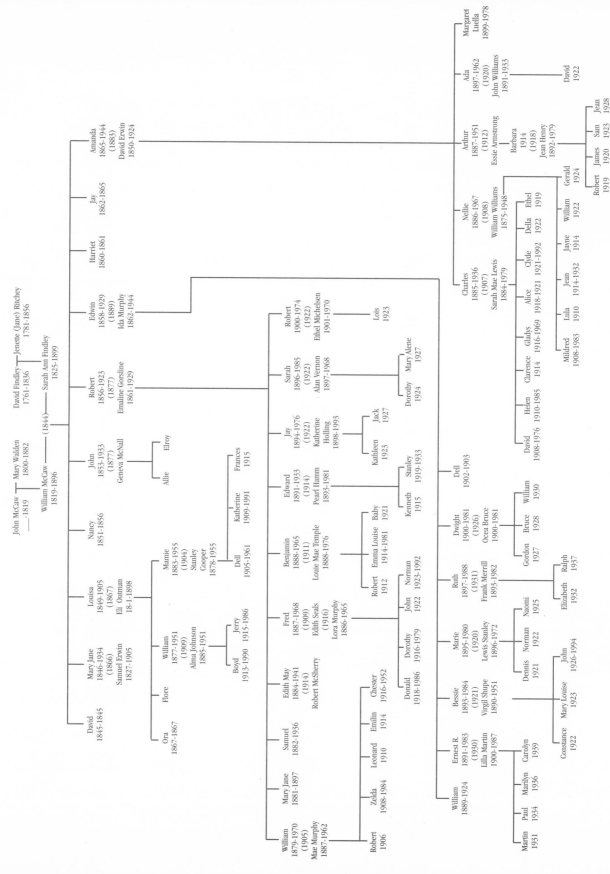

# McCaw
# Family Recipes

# Regarding The Recipes

This collection of McCaw family recipes and vignettes reflects our heritage from 1847 to 1995. It illustrates what cooking was really like during·this period and how important it was as the center of family life on the ranches and farms.

In many ways, the women in our family had special advantages because the ranches where they lived raised their own beef, dairy cattle, hogs, and poultry—and most of our families had large vegetable gardens and orchards.

Our grandmothers, mothers, and aunts were exceptionally good cooks. Although they worked hard and had large families, they enjoyed cooking, for it reflected their skill and creativity. They enjoyed many church suppers, family get-togethers, and summer picnics where they could take their favorite dishes and receive compliments. The competition among the women at these events resulted in delicious meals for everyone.

Five generations of McCaw women and their cooking are included in this book. Many of the oldest recipes are still used today, having been handed down from generation to generation, treasured for their usefulness, and adapted for modern kitchens. For each recipe presented here, the cook is identified by name and the decade of the earliest known use is noted. (For early recipes, the cook's relationship to the present generation is also noted, while recipes from our present generation are identified by the cook's name only.)

For authenticity's sake, the oldest recipes are written in their original form—in paragraphs—with the original spelling retained. The remainder are written in the style of today's cookbooks. All have been carefully tested.

A few recipes appear in more than one "version." They probably originated with Great Grandmother Sarah and were passed down to her daughters and granddaughters, each of whom adapted the original to make it her own and to use ingredients available to her. The daughters and granddaughters of my (fourth) generation are finding these old recipes fun to try as part of their own collections.

We are happy to share our family legacy with you.

# Washington Wheat
## *Our Natural Wonder*

The manicured wheat fields and hills of the Touchet Valley create a large, beautiful garden—one that the McCaw families have carefully and fruitfully tended since 1860. Touchet Valley wheat is nurtured by rich, dark volcanic loam that lies 200 to 300 feet deep on the rounded hills. Spring wheat is planted beginning in March, and by May the chartreuse of the spring wheat contrasts vividly with the dark green of winter wheat.

The pioneers brought precious wheat with them over the Oregon Trail. During their journey, they ground some to use for baking, while carefully saving some to plant in the fields of their new homes. In 1845 wheat was declared legal tender by territorial law and could be used to pay debts or acquire stoves, guns, harnesses, and other necessities. By the 1880s wheat was ground into coarse flour in the pioneers' homes or in a gristmill, if there was one nearby.

In our area, if a wheat rancher was often seen working his fields, he was considered to be a good farmer. One summer in the early 1900s Grandfather Edwin decided to have his

wheat fields in excellent condition and had the hills harrowed and rod-weeded fourteen times. This procedure left the soil like flour, and it was over ten years before it regained its original texture and its ability to hold moisture. Grandfather soon realized his mistake and encouraged other farmers not to worry about being seen working their fields!

Cousin Paul recently told me that the percentage of protein in wheat increases with the amount of stress on the growing plant. Twelve percent protein is normal, but less rain produces a higher percentage. Soft wheat, used mostly for cake flour, requires less rain than hard red spring wheat, which is marketed for bread making because of its high protein content.

After a wheat field is harvested, the land is left fallow for one year and the stubble plowed under to add nitrogen to the soil.

# Breads & Quick Breads

## Breads

## Rolls

## Quick Breads

Great Grandmother Sarah McCaw's beautiful walking spinning wheel was handcrafted for her by Josiah Osborn, her nephew. To begin, the yarn was twisted around the spindle and tied. Wool fibers are loose and stick together. While pulling the yarn and walking backwards, the spinning wheel was turned with the right hand while the yarn was drawn out with the left. When the yarn was as thin and tight as wanted the wheel was reversed to wind yarn onto the spindle. A few inches were left to attach the next piece of yarn. The wool from the full spindle was pulled off and wound onto a skein winder called a niddy-noddy. A day's spinning meant walking four or five miles!

# Narcissa Whitman's
# Camp Bread 1836

When William and Sarah finally arrived at the Whitman mission, they stayed for several weeks and were able to share fresh vegetables and fruit from the Whitmans' large garden and orchard.

Because of Great Grandmother Sarah's friendship with Narcissa Whitman this recipe is included. Camp bread was often made by the women while journeying over the Oregon Trail and was an important part of the pioneers' daily diet. This recipe was found in Narcissa Whitman's Journal. The introductory paragraph below is from the Ft. Walla Walla Museum.

*As one of the first white women to cross the Rocky Mountains, Narcissa was thrust rather unprepared into this culinary excursion. In August, 1836, Narcissa and her husband, Marcus Whitman, camped not many miles from the Snake River and in a letter to her sisters in the East, Narcissa wrote— "Girls, if you wish to know how they tasted you can have the pleasure of taking a little flour and water and make some dough, roll it thin, cut it into square blocks then take some beef fat and fry them. You need not put either salt or pearl ash on your dough. Believe me, I relish these as well as I ever did any made at home.*

The Museum at Fort Walla Walla displays the recipe below on a large card beside our Great Grandmother Sarah's spinning wheel, in the Marcus Whitman exhibit.

One cup flour mixed with one half cup water
Bacon or beef fat for frying.

For our modern tastes: Add 1½ teaspoons baking powder and ½ teaspoon salt. Stir, then knead until free from lumps. Roll or pat ½ inch thick. Cut into 2-inch squares and fry over medium heat until lightly browned. Turn and cook on the other side. When done place on paper towels to drain a little and serve warm.

Note: Pearl ash was early-day baking powder made from wood ashes. I tried Narcissa's recipe and the modern version, frying them in a very old cast iron skillet with bacon drippings, and found both to be delicious.

*Journal of Narcissa Whitman*
*Courtesy of Fort Walla Walla Museum and the Bancroft Library*

# Grandmother Amanda McCaw Erwin's
# Communion Bread   1800s

Della Mae writes: "Amanda baked this for the Prescott Presbyterian Church for a number of years. I made it for Walla Walla Presbyterian and my sister Joy Erwin baked it regularly for the College Place Presbyterian. I believe it is still used there."

1 cup flour
⅓ cup lard
⅛ cup sugar
Pinch of salt
Milk

Mix all except milk, then add just enough to make like pie dough. Roll it, score it, prick it with fork to look like cracker. Bake it in 350 degree oven about 10-15 minutes until it has a light brown look. Break in pieces when cool.

*Della Mae Erwin Sanders*

16

# Grandmother Amanda McCaw Erwin's
## Steamed Bread   1880s

There is the family story that Great Grandmother Sarah took her bread starter to bed with her every night to keep it warm and "working." The starter was poured into a jar with a tight lid, then wrapped in a towel and tucked into her bed. With little yeast available it was necessary to keep the starter going. The women with large families baked bread nearly every day and kept their starter active for months, even years. Coming across the Oregon Trail, the pioneers found that the bread starter was a very important part of their daily lives. It provided the only means to bake bread for all the families and was sometimes kept right in the sack of flour. For each baking, enough starter and flour would be mixed in a bowl or pan, leaving some starter to increase for the next baking.

2½ cups sour milk

1½ cups corn meal

1½ cups graham flour

2 cups white flour

⅔ cup molasses

1 teaspoon soda

Add 1 cup raisins if you prefer. Pour mixture into 1-pound coffee cans or smaller. Cover with brown paper and tie with string. Place cans on rack in large kettle with hot water added to cover ½ sides of cans. Steam 3 hours.

Jane Lust Williams' Note: To sour the milk add 1 Tablespoon lemon juice and stir. Recipe makes two 1-pound coffee cans. Cans should be well greased. When done, let stand 10 minutes then loosen sides and shake out of can. Very good served with baked beans.

*Della Mae Erwin Sanders*

# Grandmother Ida McCaw's
## Potato Bread   1890s

Note from Mary Shupe McCarthy: "I imagine this was a recipe Grandma used for years, making 4-6 loaves at a time. Since every woman had to bake all the bread her family ate, each knew the techniques, how much flour to add, how to judge the proper rising time, etc. I can imagine Aunt Ruth pressing her for the recipe and taking notes as Grandma remembered it. It probably would have been perfectly clear to every woman of her generation, but it wasn't to me. I guessed at 2 cups liquid, added a second package of yeast for good measure and stopped counting at 10 cups of flour. I think Grandma's recipe has a lot of charm. I can imagine her voice as she explained how simple it was.

Original Recipe:
Take three or four good size potatoes. Boil, when done, mash, put back into water. When cool drop in yeast cake. Let stand til light then add enough flour to make it a thick batter to rise again. When light mix stiff and rise, then put in pan. Bake at 375-400 degrees.

*Ruth McCaw Merrill*

Updated Version:

        1½ cups cooked potatoes, unseasoned

        2 Tablespoons sugar

        3 teaspoons salt

        1 cup water potatoes were cooked in plus 1 cup water

        2 packages yeast

        ⅓ cup very warm water

        6 cups flour, approximately

        2-4 Tablespoons melted butter or shortening

Mash the hot potatoes. Add potato water and additional water. When mixture is lukewarm add the yeast which has been dissolved in the very warm water. Stir in 3 cups flour and beat until smooth. Gradually add flour to make a medium stiff dough. Turn dough onto a lightly floured board and knead until dough is smooth and elastic. Place in a greased bowl: turn over to lightly grease top of dough. Cover and let rise in a warm place until doubled in size. Punch down. Divide dough in half, then cover with a cloth for 10 minutes. Shape into loaves and place in greased loaf pans. Cover and let rise until doubled in size. Bake in 400 degree oven for 10 minutes then reduce heat to 350 degrees. Bake 40-45 minutes until lightly brown on top. Cool on rack for 10 minutes and remove from pans.

Note: Potatoes absorb the salty flavor; you can add 1-2 teaspoons more salt if you like. When loaves come out of the oven, take one half cube of butter or margarine, leaving it in the paper with part of the cube exposed. Hold gently and rub over the top and sides of each loaf of bread. This produces a softer crust with a delicious buttery, salty flavor.

*Mary Shupe McCarthy*

# Grandmother Mae McCaw's
# Boston Brown Bread   1910s

Grandmother had a coal and wood stove on the farm, where she cooked for the ranch hands during harvest. She baked all the bread, churned the butter, and was busy all day creating large meals for the workers and her family. This recipe was one of her "crowd pleasers."

Combine:

  1 cup whole wheat flour

  1 cup white flour

  2 cups wheat germ

  2 cups fruit (raisins)

  1 cup nuts (if desired)

  1 round teaspoon salt

  2 level teaspoons baking soda dissolved in 2 full cups buttermilk

  12-ounce bottle molasses (I prefer Grandma's brand)

Steam 3 hours covered in well-greased 1-pound coffee cans. Uncover and dry off in slow oven for 15 minutes or so. Cool on rack and store in cool place in cans.

Updated Version:
On top of stove, in a covered container large enough to accommodate three 1-pound cans, place the filled coffee tins. (Use aluminum foil to cover cans tightly and tie with string).

Add water to container so that coffee tins are submerged half way. Place lid on kettle. Bring water to boil. Keep water at a boil for 3 hours, over medium heat, replacing water as necessary. Uncover and dry off in 325 degree oven for 15 minutes or so. Cool on rack, and store in cool place in cans. Can be frozen, but remove from cans and wrap well first.

*Jerrianne McCaw Powell*

*1918. Ethel McCaw at the spring breakup of ice on the Touchet River.*

# Bessie McCaw Shupe's
# Salt Rising Bread   1920s

In 1992 cousin Mary Shupe McCarthy sent notes on her adventures in baking: "I've spent three weekends baking bread and have sixteen loaves of bread to show for it. Since I've become addicted to the memory of good Salt Rising Bread I'm not going to give up until I have a foolproof method of making that elusive perfect loaf!

When cousin Dorothea sent her recipe to me, she ended with "Good Luck!" It's no wonder that pioneer women were excited and delighted when they were successful with this bread. It was a great event in our house! Grandma Mary Ella Shupe told of wrapping the starter in an old Mason Jar with blankets and taking it to bed to keep it warm and working."

Original Recipe Starter:

>   4 teaspoons corn meal
>
>   ¼ teaspoon sugar
>
>   ¼ teaspoon soda
>
>   Pinch of ginger

Milk scant pint, bring to boiling point, cool a little. Add other ingredients. Let set in kettle of water. Have the water hot enough to just hold hand in. Pour hot milk over this and put to rise for 18 to 24 hours until bubbles rise. Make sponge by adding to Starter one quart milk or water, ½ teaspoon sugar, ¼ teaspoon soda, a little more ginger, and 1 Tablespoon salt. Add 4 cups flour to make moderately thick batter and again set in pan of warm water. Leave until bubbles work up from bottom, about 2 hours. Stir in flour to make soft, not stiff, dough and knead. Shape into loaves. Let double in bulk and bake.

Mary's 1992 Version of Starter:

>   4 Tablespoons non-degerminated cornmeal
>
>   1 teaspoon sugar
>
>   ¼ teaspoon baking soda
>
>   Pinch of ginger—scant ⅛ teaspoon

Scald 1½ cups milk. Cool slightly and pour over above ingredients. Put in a jar or non-metallic bowl, cover and set in a pan of hot water. Keep at a warm temperature until it bubbles and is frothy. This can take 18 to 24 hours. The most successful method I have found to get a starter is the use of a Crockpot with a ceramic liner. I start it around 7 p.m. and set it at the lowest temperature—around 120 degrees—and leave it all night. I watch it closely when I arise in the morning to determine when it bubbles up from the bottom.

When bubbles rise, add fermented mixture to:

      4 cups very warm water

      3 teaspoons sugar

      ¼ teaspoon baking soda

      1 Tablespoon salt

      Pinch of ginger—scant ⅛ teaspoon

Add 6 cups flour to make a moderately thick batter. Set in pan of warm water and leave until bubbles work up from bottom. Stir in additional flour to make soft, not stiff, dough. It should just be able to be handled. Knead several minutes until elastic. Shape into 3 loaves and place in well greased bread pans. Lightly grease the tops of loaves with Crisco vegetable shortening, to prevent hard crusts forming. Bread tends to get a hard crust on top which impedes rising, I believe. I lightly greased the tops of loaves after I placed them in pans, and I think it allowed the dough to stretch easier, hence rise more. Let double in bulk in a warm place and bake at 375 degrees for 10 minutes. Reduce heat to 350 degrees and bake 25-30 minutes longer until lightly browned. Cool on rack for 10 minutes and remove loaves from pans. If you like, while loaves are still hot take a cube of butter or margarine and rub all surfaces generously. This gives a buttery crust. The intriguing flavor is wonderful when bread is toasted, with orange marmalade.

A constant medium hot temperature is the key to success with this bread. Recommended in various recipes are the top of a water heater, the back of a wood stove, or an oven (if you keep adding boiling water to keep the temperature from lowering). I tried setting the bowl on a trivet in a Sunbeam frying pan with ½ inch of water in the bottom, left it on the lowest temperature, watched it carefully, and kept turning the control off and on all day.

It is impossible to get a starter from degerminated cornmeal. One can buy the non-degerminated kind at health stores and at some supermarkets which sell in the bulk.

*Mary Shupe McCarthy and Connie Shupe Plants*

# Fragrances
# In Our Valley

Pussywillows, pungent in early March
Hyacinths and daffodils
Appleblossoms—the best of all
Newly plowed earth in spring
Beautiful wild Syringa along the Touchet River
so fragrant we could always tell when it was in bloom
Locust trees in blossom, creating perfumed white clouds
Wild rose on the old fence down the lane
Phlox on a warm summer evening and
Alyssum on hot summer afternoons
Tomatoes in August
Freshly mown alfalfa with purple blossoms
The mellow scent of ripe fruit—
Warm, fuzzy peaches
Blackberries
Ripe pears
Sun-warmed apples in their wooden boxes, Fresh cider
Pungent sage in October
Smoky bonfires where we cooked potatoes wrapped in leaves.

# Grandmother Emma Holling's
## Kuchen   1930s

Kathleen writes: "Grandmother enjoyed making this traditional family coffee cake for her family and ours."

> ¾ cup lukewarm milk
>
> ¼ cup sugar
>
> 1 package yeast
>
> 1 large egg
>
> ¼ cup soft shortening
>
> 2¼ cups sifted flour
>
> ½ teaspoon mace
>
> ⅛ teaspoon nutmeg

Mix together milk, sugar, and yeast. When dissolved add slightly beaten egg and melted shortening. Add flour and spices. Beat batter for 1 minute. Cover and let rise about 1½ hours. Beat well. Shape in a ring and put in a greased 9-inch round cake pan. Sprinkle on Streusel topping. Let rise about 45 minutes. Bake at 350 degrees for 30-35 minutes. Serve warm.

Streusel topping:
> ¼ cup brown sugar
>
> 1 teaspoon cinnamon
>
> 2 Tablespoons flour
>
> 2 Tablespoons soft butter

Mix ingredients until crumbly.

*Kathleen McCaw Bergevin*

# Golden Apricot Bread   1990s

Occasionally, a family of coyotes will develop a taste for watermelons or other fruit and help themselves. However, for reasons no one understands, coyotes never break open a watermelon that is not perfectly ripe. In 1979 Carolyn Houger, a granddaughter of the original Prescott McCaws, witnessed a spectacular exhibition of fruit picking, when a family of coyotes came up from the Touchet River at dusk and descended on the Houger's backyard apricot tree. The apricots, newly ripe, had not yet fallen to the ground, so the coyotes entertained Carolyn and her family with a 15-minute exhibition of vertical high jumping, as they leaped for the lower branches to gather their dinner.

*Written by Paul McCaw*

Sourdough starter is used today, as it was 150 years ago. Sometimes in spring, summer, and fall, a jar of milk without a lid would be set outside for a day or longer to catch the "wild yeast." This would create a sourdough starter that could be used indefinitely. I tried this years ago and found that it does work! I now use a similar procedure for baking Golden Apricot Bread, placing the bowl of starter on my kitchen counter all day or overnight to create that wonderful sourdough fragrance and flavor.

Starter:

      1 Tablespoon active dry yeast (1 envelope)

      2 cups unsifted unbleached flour

      3½ Tablespoons sugar

      1 teaspoon salt

      2 cups warm water, 112-115 degrees

In a large bowl stir together all dry ingredients. Add warm water and gently whisk until well blended. Cover bowl with dish towel and leave on the counter during the day, until bubbly. Stir several times. Refrigerate overnight. Remove and let starter come to room temperature. When ready to bake follow directions below.

To Bake:

Set oven at 350 degrees. Recipe makes 3 nice loaves in 7½ x 3½-inch pans. Gently stir starter and measure 1½-1¾ cups for baking. Set aside remainder of starter.

Add:    2 cups unbleached flour

2 small boxes Instant Vanilla pudding mix

⅔ cup sugar

½ teaspoon salt

½+ teaspoon baking soda, ¼+ teaspoon baking powder

1 Tablespoon cinnamon

1 cup Wesson oil

½ cup 2% milk

3 eggs slightly beaten

1 Tablespoon Schilling Pure Vanilla Extract

1 cup raisins

1 cup broken walnuts

9 ounces dried apricots (1½ packages Sunsweet Dried Apricots), quartered. I stack 4 apricot halves to quarter them, making them easier to cut with a knife.

Mix all dry ingredients in a bowl. Mix all liquid ingredients in another bowl. Combine raisins, walnuts, and apricots. At this point cut parchment to fit bottom of each pan and grease sides of loaf pans with Crisco shortening. Coat sides with sugar. Add about 1 Tablespoon sugar to each pan to evenly coat bottom. This extra sugar helps the bread release easily when baked. Add dry and liquid ingredients to starter and mix with a wooden spoon or large plastic coated wire whip. Add fruit and nuts last. Divide into three pans and bake 50 minutes in center of oven (check with wooden skewer for doneness). Cool for 10 minutes on rack, then loosen bread from pan by running a table knife around edges and invert to cool topside up on racks. Serve warm or cold. Slices can be reheated about 20 seconds in microwave. This delicious bread freezes well.

To the remaining starter add:

1 cup unbleached flour

1 cup 2% milk

⅔ cup sugar

Mix gently until well blended with large plastic coated wire whip or wooden spoon. Leave starter on counter for 8-12 hours until bubbly, then cover and refrigerate.

*Naomi and Pat and John Sawyer*

*In the early 1880s Frank T. Gilbert published historic sketches by A. Burr of many farms in Walla Walla County, including Great Uncle Sam and Great Aunt Mary Erwin's farm near the Touchet River and Prescott. His fruit and nut orchard was well established at that time.*

# Grandmother Emma McCaw's
## Parker House Rolls   1800s

Cousin Alene Bedford writes: "The Bruce House in Waitsburg is a fine Historical Museum with much information about early wheat farming. On a wall there is an impressive handmade quilt with this story: 'In World War I the flour mills in Waitsburg heard about a village in Belgium where the people were starving. They sent sacks of wheat and flour to the village. As a Thank You to the people of Waitsburg, the Belgian women made a large quilt and sent it to the mills there. Sewn into the quilt are the flour sacks from the Waitsburg mills.' "

1 egg

½ cup butter

1 teaspoon salt

½ cup sugar

1 yeast cake

3 cups warm water

1 teaspoon baking powder

7 cups flour

In bowl place yeast, 1 cup warm water, and 1 Tablespoon sugar. Let yeast mixture rise. Sift flour. Mix salt, sugar, and baking powder in with the flour. Add egg, melted butter, water, yeast mixture, and flour. Turn out on bread board and knead. Put in greased bowl and let double in size. Shape into rolls and place in greased baking pan and let rise. Bake at 400 degrees for 15-20 minutes.

*Lois McCaw Ellsaesser*

# Nellie Erwin Williams'
# Yeast Muffin Pan Rolls   1920s

Jane comments "These delicious muffins can be made for Sunday dinner even after attending church."

1 cup milk

2 Tablespoons sugar

1 teaspoon salt

2 Tablespoons shortening

1 cake yeast

¼ cup lukewarm water

2 eggs, beaten

2½ cups flour

Scald milk, add sugar, salt, and shortening. Dissolve yeast in warm water and add to milk mixture. Add well-beaten eggs and flour. Beat until smooth. Let rise until light (about 1 hour). Fill greased muffin pans about ⅔ full. Let rise again about ½ hour until very light. Bake in a moderate oven, 350 degrees for 20-25 minutes.

*Jane and Bill Williams*

# Lilla McCaw's
# "Light as a Feather" Dinner Rolls   1930s

When the women spent hours each day in their kitchens, they found time to be creative and to take advantage of the abundance of summer's fresh fruit and vegetables and year-round dairy products. While baking bread or cakes they often cooked other dishes, canned fruit, or made jelly, jam, and pickles. Skill was required to bake in the ovens of the old wood ranges. The temperature was controlled by adding another piece of wood at just the right time. Before thermometers were added to the oven door, the women would open the oven to feel the temperature. Surprisingly, almost everything they baked turned out to be delicious!

When we were invited to dinner, it was delightful to be greeted by the yeasty fragrance of Aunt Lilla's special rolls, ready for the oven.

> 3 cups milk
> 4 Tablespoons sugar
> 4 teaspoons salt
> 1 cup Crisco
> 8½ cups flour
> 4 eggs

Mix first four ingredients and scald together, then cool. When tepid, add 3 cakes or 3 packages dry yeast (moistened in a little warm water), and well-beaten eggs. Measure flour by gently spooning it into a measuring cup. Add flour until a soft dough is formed, but not too soft to handle. If the dough is quite soft, add a little more flour as you knead it on the board. Return to well greased pot or original dish. Let rise till light. Roll out about ½ inch thick and cut in circles with biscuit or doughnut cutter about 3 inches in diameter. With table knife gently crease in center and fold over. Let rise again and bake at 400 degrees 15 to 20 minutes.

Note: Crisco was first marketed in 1911 and was a welcome new shortening for cakes and pies, producing a lighter texture and flavor.

*Paul McCaw, Carolyn McCaw Houger, and Marilyn McCaw Griffin*

# Vignettes of Spring

In March, when the hills were being seeded with spring wheat, at night we would hear the tractors and see their floodlights slowly moving over the ground. Seeding continued around the clock until the work was completed.

We enjoyed the frogs' croaking in their celebration of spring and searching for pollywogs in rain puddles along the road.

Clothes hung on the line billowed straight out in welcome, strong, warm winds giving them a fresh, wonderful fragrance. It was a joy to bring in an armful.

When grandfather Edwin had a large flock of sheep grazing on the hills, he would ride over on his horse with his favorite sheepdog standing behind his saddle. He was remarkably well trained. At grandfather's signal Shep would cover each hill at a run, bringing in the entire flock by himself while grandfather waited. Some of the flocks were half a mile away.

# Grandmother Ida McCaw's
# Cream Fried Cakes   1890s

When Grandmother was a young woman living in the Willamette Valley in Oregon Territory, she rode horseback to teach in a little schoolhouse up in the Cascade Mountains. Later, she married Edwin McCaw and in 1896 they moved to the Touchet Valley in Washington Territory. Before she left her home in Oregon, she gathered recipes like this one from family and friends. These interesting cakes are really free-form doughnuts and very delicious. Fun for young people to make for a party.

> 1 cup sour cream
> 1 cup buttermilk
> 1 teaspoon baking soda
> 2 eggs
> 1 cup sugar
> 3½ cups flour

Flavor with nutmeg. Add a pinch of ginger to prevent them from absorbing the grease. Flour to make a soft dough.

Updated version:
Beat eggs, add sugar and mix. Add sour cream and buttermilk, stirring gently. Flavor with 2 teaspoons nutmeg and a pinch of ginger. Add spices and baking soda to flour. Next add the flour mixture and stir until the batter is well blended and you have a soft dough. Drop by Tablespoonsful into hot shortening. Brown on one side and turn over with a slotted spoon. When done, drain on paper towels, serve plain, or coat with sugar by shaking in a paper bag that has sugar added. Enjoy while warm with cider, coffee, or milk.

Note: Crisco vegetable shortening is the best to use, I believe, and makes a delicious doughnut-like treat. Freshly grated nutmeg adds the best flavor.

*Ruth McCaw Merrill*

# Grandmother Ida McCaw's
# Puff Ball Doughnuts  1890s

Doughnuts were enjoyed all year, but they were made most often in the fall, usually in October and November. Doughnut and cider-making parties were fun for families and friends up and down the valley. Great quantities of cider were made on Grandfather Edwin's cider press, an antique press that was rebuilt by cousin Paul McCaw and each October is the center of attention at cider-making parties at his farm.

Grandfather was known throughout the valley for his fine orchard. He and Great Uncle Sam Erwin owned the largest commercial orchards in the valley. Grandfather hybridized many varieties of apples and plums. Apple harvest meant hard work—sometimes over 1,000 boxes of apples would be picked in one season. The red delicious apples were the old variety, with their wonderful flavor, always cold and crisp to pick from the trees and enjoy.

2¾ cups sour cream and ¼ cup milk

2 cups sugar

3 large or extra large eggs

1 teaspoon baking soda

1½ teaspoons baking powder

2 Tablespoons fresh grated nutmeg

1 Tablespoon vanilla

2 teaspoons salt

6 cups flour, sifted and measured

Beat eggs until light. Add sugar and vanilla and mix well. Add flour, baking soda, baking powder, salt, and nutmeg. Stir well, making a soft dough. Turn out on a floured bread board, rolling gently or patting dough until it is about ¾ inch thick. Cut with a doughnut cutter and drop two or three at one time into hot melted Crisco vegetable shortening. Turn when browned and cook on the other side. Remove and drain on paper towels. If you like, place each one on a plate covered with sugar, turning to coat both sides. Children have fun shaking the hot doughnuts in a small paper sack to coat with sugar. This is the old-fashioned way that we remember. The doughnut holes are still favorites of the children.

*Ruth McCaw Merrill*

# Marie McCaw Stanley's
# Honey Biscuits   1920s

This was a favorite in our family and my first try at baking when I was seven or eight years old. Always a success, it created my interest in cooking. Of course, we made our own biscuit dough from scratch. Our grandmothers and mothers often made their biscuits with sour cream and bacon grease for shortening. They were wonderful!

Butter or margarine
Honey
2 cups Jiffy Biscuit Mix
¾ cup milk

Heat oven to 350 degrees. Place 1 Tablespoon of butter or margarine in each cup of a muffin pan. Put in oven for a minute or two to melt. Remove muffin pan from oven. Add 1 Tablespoon honey to each muffin cup. Mix biscuit dough as for drop biscuits, then add a heaping Tablespoon of biscuit dough to each cup. (It should make the muffin cup about one-half full). Bake 15-18 minutes. The longer they are baked the more sticky they become. When the bubbles around the edge of the muffin cups disappear, the biscuits are done. When removed from oven, immediately hold a cookie sheet over the muffin pan and invert both. Honey biscuits will fall out of the muffin pan onto the cookie sheet. Spoon out the remaining syrup with a Tablespoon. Serve hot, with butter or margarine if desired.

*Naomi*

# Happy Birthday Dinner
## for Alene & Dorothy Vernon
### 1920s & 1930s

Chicken stew with dumplings

Home canned green peas

Home grown potatoes, mashed

Home canned pear salad with grated Tillamook cheese

Homemade Angel Food Cake (the egg whites were whisked by hand and the
     cake baked in a wood stove oven—they always came out perfect)

Homemade Ice Cream, hand cranked in the old wooden freezer

On the farm we had chickens, lots of eggs, and cream. The cheese for the salad was the only thing from the store. Oh, and the ice to make the ice cream. In the winter when the river was frozen we would bring back ice and make ice cream in front of the big fireplace.

When we were children, my sister and I had our birthday dinner together since our birthdays were March 2 and 8. We always had lots of cousins, friends from school, and teachers come out to the farm for the day. My father loaded all of us in the flatbed wagon and the horses pulled us across the Touchet River over to the hills to pick wild flowers. When we arrived home we all ran into the house with our arms full of wild flowers and presented them to Mother. Ah, the aroma of chicken and dumplings as we washed up for our memorable dinner.

*Alene Vernon Bedford*

Ethel adds: "I remember the beautiful Locust trees lining the lane from our house to the county road. In June there was that wonderful aroma of Locust blossoms. They were almost as thick as snow. And hanging from the branches were dozens of Baltimore Oriole nests. Our house and farm was very well known for many miles around as Locust Lane."

*1930. Dorothy and Alene Vernon's birthday party excursion across the Touchet River to pick wildflowers on the hills. From left to right are Alan Vernon, Dorothy Vernon, Lois Pollard, Helen Rector, Dick Holling, Lois McCaw, Naomi Stanley, Kathleen McCaw, Jack McCaw, Alene Vernon, Hazel Harkins, Doris Pollard, Jane Pollard, Norman McCaw, LeRoy Pollard, and John McCaw.*

# Marie McCaw Stanley's
## Sunday Night Waffles   1920s

Our nearest neighbor and dear friend, Nora Hopwood, baked bread and rolls nearly every day of the year for her husband and four sons. A large jar of starter sat on her kitchen windowsill. Made of potato water, it made the best sourdough I can remember, and what a heady fragrance. When on horseback in the early afternoon I'd ride to Nora's kitchen where she would be baking her delicious rolls. She always shared some hot out of the oven. I'm certain that I was expected often, for she was never surprised to see me. Sometimes she would play favorite songs on her piano, giving warm, happy memories to cherish today. Nora's family enjoyed Mother's waffle suppers with us, with home cured ham, bacon, and home made maple syrup. Fifty years later it's fun to know that waffles are still a favorite for Sunday night suppers.

> 1½ cups flour
>
> 2 teaspoons baking powder
>
> ½ teaspoon salt
>
> ¼ cup melted butter
>
> 1 Tablespoon sugar
>
> 1 cup milk
>
> 2 eggs

Mix flour, baking powder, salt, and sugar together. Add milk and melted butter. Add beaten egg yolks. Then gently fold in the stiffly beaten egg whites. With a pastry brush lightly coat hot waffle iron with cooking oil to prevent waffles sticking.

*Naomi*

# Marie McCaw Stanley's
# Home Made Maple Syrup

2 cups brown sugar

1 cup water

1 teaspoon maple flavoring

Boil the sugar and water for 3-5 minutes. Remove from heat and add maple flavoring. Serve warm over waffles and pancakes.

*Naomi*

# Marie McCaw Stanley's
# Campfire Doughgods   1930s

In the summer we would often hike the half mile down the lane to the Touchet River for a picnic and swimming. Before we left the house, Mother would prepare a dry biscuit mix that we would take along. Water or milk would be added and pieces of dough rolled in our hands to make ropes about 1 inch thick and 8 inches long. My brothers cut and peeled the bark from straight green branches about an inch thick and we would wind the dough around each branch. Then we would hold the sticks over the campfire until the dough was baked. Your children can pretend they are pioneers while they try these around your next campfire.

Note: Try this using a prepared biscuit mix. 2 cups biscuit mix, ½ cup milk. A stiff dough is required to roll nicely and hold its shape. Divide the dough in 8 pieces and roll each one 8-10 inches long. Flatten, then wrap around the stick in a spiral, starting at the end of the stick. Press ends lightly to adhere to stick. Toast slowly over campfire coals until browned and puffed. Enjoy while hot with lots of fresh butter, margarine, or honey butter.

Honey Butter:

> Mix softened butter with your favorite honey until it tastes just the way you like best. Spread on hot, floury biscuits around your campfire or right out of the oven.

*Naomi*

# Hop Yeast

Hops are grown on many acres in the Willamette Valley in Oregon and the Yakima River Valley in Washington.

This very old recipe for making yeast in the 1800s enabled more women to do their own baking when they didn't have yeast from the store. It would be worth a try when you're exploring new methods of baking bread.

Boil two ounces of best hops in four quarts water for half an hour. Strain and cool till lukewarm. Add small handful salt and half pound sugar, one pound Snowdrift flour, and part of liquid. Beat together well. The third day add three pounds mashed potatoes. Let stand till next day. Strain and boil, then it is ready for use. Stir frequently while making and keep near fire. Shake before using.

*Ladies of the Presbyterian Church Cookbook, Prescott, 1903*

*1930s. Dennis, Norman, and Naomi Stanley enjoy a lazy summer afternoon.*

# Simple Pleasures

Our valley was exciting to explore. As children and young adults we could wander wherever we wanted. Sometimes we would ride horses to the crest of the highest hill, usually in the stubble after harvest. From this vantage point we could see the gigantic water gap on the Columbia River forty miles away as it makes the bend toward the West, just south of the site of Old Fort Walla Walla, which stood there 150 years ago.

Other afternoons were spent climbing fruit trees and hanging by our knees at a height that made our mothers shudder. The apple tree bark was smooth and the limbs were spaced just right for easy climbing.

Another favorite activity was walking the high, narrow beams in our huge barn before jumping down into the hay. Sometimes we were joined by our cousins who lived nearby. A long rope high up in the top of the barn was attached to the carriage for bringing in the hay, just under the cupola. It made a grand swing from one loft to the other. If you didn't swing far enough to reach the other side, you eventually had to let go and fall into the hay below. Sometimes it was a long, long way down!

Quite a few afternoons were spent with our cousins, building bonfires and roasting apples until they were blackened on the outside and hot and juicy inside.

Sailing simple, little homemade boats down the irrigation stream that ran from the river around the base of the hills kept us busy on hot summer days.

Children and young adults created their own fun most of the time. Climbing trees; swimming and fishing in the Touchet River; exploring everywhere; riding horseback; playing with the baby animals; going on hay rides, sleigh rides, and picnics; attending box suppers, ice cream socials, dances, and potluck suppers for the family and the community—these were just some of the many activities we enjoyed while growing up.

# Salads, Soups, & Side Dishes

## Salads

## Soups

## Side Dishes & Accompaniments

# Grandmother Amanda McCaw Erwin's
# Cream Slaw with Hot Dressing   1890s

This salad must have been prepared for the harvest crew, usually fifteen to twenty men. And we did have larger families then!

One gallon cabbage cut very fine, pint of vinegar, pint sour cream, half cup sugar, teaspoon Snowdrift flour, two eggs, and a piece of butter the size of a walnut. Put vinegar, sugar, and butter in a sauce pan and let boil. Stir eggs, cream, and flour, previously well mixed, into the vinegar. Boil thoroughly, and throw over the cabbage previously sprinkled with a tea-spoonful of salt, one of black pepper, one of mustard.

Note: This recipe can be cut in half or less—interesting for creative cooks to try!

*Ladies of the Presbyterian Church Cookbook, Prescott, 1903*

# Grandmother Amanda McCaw Erwin's
## Everyday Salad Dressing   1890s

Every ranch raised its own chickens, and sometimes ducks and geese. Eggs were plentiful and several dozen could be used in a day, for breakfast, cooking, and baking.

The yolks of eleven eggs, one cup of vinegar, one of water, three-fourths cup of sugar, one-half cup butter, one teaspoonful of salt and one Tablespoon of dry mustard. Beat the yolks of eggs well and add other ingredients and cook in double boiler until thickened. Try with Grandmother Ida McCaw's Lobster Salad.

*Ladies of the Presbyterian Church Cookbook, Prescott, 1903*

# Grandmother Ida McCaw's
## Lobster Salad   July 4, 1896

One small cabbage chopped fine, one onion chopped fine, 3 sour pickles chopped coarsely, add can of lobster and three hard boiled eggs.
Mix and chill.

*Naomi*

*1929. A summertime visit from our Corvallis cousins meant exploring the ranch. Grandmother Ida McCaw almost escaped the photographer. Cousins from head to tail are John Shupe, Norman and Naomi Stanley, a friend, Mary Louise and Connie Shupe, and Dennis Stanley.*

# Grandmother Ida McCaw's
# Cream Dressing for Cole Slaw   1920s

This was a favorite salad dressing in both summer and winter.

2 Tablespoons whipping cream
2 Tablespoons sugar
4 Tablespoons cider vinegar
Chunk pineapple

Beat well and pour over very fine shredded cabbage that has been seasoned with salt. Pineapple adds a fresh flavor and texture.

Note: Did you know the word "cole" means cabbage?

*Naomi*

# Peach Cups
## with Apple Butter   1920s

Great Uncle Sam Erwin, recognized for his very large orchard, grew peaches and other fruit to perfection. This article from *The Waitsburg Times*, October 11, 1889 tells one story: "Samuel H. Erwin, of Prescott, carried off thirteen First prizes and six Second prizes for fruit displayed at our Walla Walla County Fair. He also got the $10.00 special prize given by Henry Kelling for the finest general display exhibited by the producer." He would have enjoyed this salad made from a favorite fruit, then and now.

12 canned cling peach halves

¼ cup chopped walnuts

¼ cup finely chopped celery

¼ cup seeded raisins

3 Tablespoons apple butter

Best Foods mayonnaise

Arrange nests of lettuce on individual plates. In each nest place one peach half. Grind raisins. Combine celery, nuts, raisins and apple butter. Generously fill each peach half. Top each with a teaspoon mayonnaise.

*Home Economics Club Cookbook, Prescott, 1942*

# Marie McCaw Stanley's
# Rosy Cinnamon Apples   1930s

These bright red apples were a Thanksgiving and Christmas tradition in our family. The red and green are pretty on the table. This last Thanksgiving, 1992, I shared them with our cousins and found that Aunt Lilla McCaw made dozens of them for church suppers at Prescott at holiday time, and they were also a Thanksgiving tradition in her home. This is an old family recipe, cherished by Bessie, Ruth, and Marie's families.

2½ cups red cinnamon candies, tiny round hard ones

5⅓ cups water

2½ cups sugar

12 small Rome apples pared, cored, and halved

Red food coloring

Quite small Rome apples can be cooked whole, if you can find them. Dissolve candies in boiling water, stirring constantly to prevent sticking. Add sugar and stir to dissolve. Add red food coloring for a nice dark red apple. Add several halves of apples and simmer until tender when pricked with a dinner fork. Cook with the round side up for about two minutes then turn over and continue cooking, usually about 6-8 more minutes. Gently lift apples from syrup and place in a large glass Pyrex baking pan. Cool syrup, then pour over apples and refrigerate overnight. Serve on lettuce with a teaspoon of Best Foods mayonnaise and a teaspoon of chopped walnuts sprinkled on top.

Note: Apples at room temperature will cook more quickly than cold ones. As you peel and core apples, place in a bowl of warm water to keep from darkening. The warm water will help them cook nicely too.

*Naomi*

# Ethel Michelsen McCaw's
## Frozen Slaw Salad   1930s

Gelatin salads were cool and refreshing. Cabbage was plentiful and by the early 1930s our farms had refrigerators with freezer compartments.

1 Tablespoon gelatine dissolved in ¼ cup water

2 cups shredded cabbage

1 cup crushed pineapple

¼ cup pineapple juice

¼ cup sugar

½ teaspoon salt

½ cup mayonnaise

¾ cup whipped cream

Put ingredients together in the above order and place in refrigerator tray or glass pan. Freeze until firm. Slice and serve on lettuce leaf. Excellent with turkey or steak.

*Lois McCaw Ellsaesser*

# Allie Kinder Neal's
# Rice Delight Fruit Salad   1930s

Allie Kinder, my friend from the first grade in Prescott, recently shared this recipe with me. Allie's Aunt Nancy brought this interesting salad to family holiday dinners and celebrations long ago. Today her children and grandchildren request their favorite Rice Salad when they arrive for those special dinners.

Mix and refrigerate until cold:

      1 cup white rice, cooked, drained and cooled (equals 2 cups cooked)

      8 slices canned pineapple, cut in chunks

      1 apple, cut in ½ inch cubes

      2 small cans green grapes, drained

      2 small cans mandarin oranges, drained

Just before serving add:

      2 medium bananas, sliced

      1 Tablespoon sugar

      1 Tablespoon Schilling Pure Vanilla Extract

      1 cup whipping cream, measured and whipped with sugar and vanilla

Gently fold whipped cream into fruit and serve in lettuce cups. The rice creates an interesting and unexpected texture.

*Naomi*

*"Life goes on—This picture was taken in the early 1930s at the ranch near Prescott. In the background is the house where I was born. In the foreground is the combine pulled by 21 horses. This machine had five men working on it." —W. P. Williams*

# Marie McCaw Stanley's
# Hot Chicken Salad   1950s

Mother and her sister Bessie Shupe enjoyed this special salad at a potluck luncheon at their sorority reunion in Corvallis, Oregon. On the back of the recipe card I found this note: "This hot chicken salad was the best dish there!"

Mix in saucepan:

      2 cups cooked chicken, light and dark meat cut in 1 inch cubes

      2 cups thinly sliced celery

      ½ cup chopped toasted almonds

      ½ teaspoon salt

      1 Tablespoon grated onion

      1 cup Best Foods mayonnaise

      2 Tablespoons fresh lemon juice

      ½ cup grated sharp cheddar cheese

      Potato chips

Mix gently and place on medium low heat to warm slowly. Stir. When hot, spoon into low casserole dish. Sprinkle with grated cheese and crushed potato chips. Heat in oven 10 minutes at 450 degrees. Serve at once.

Note: Because this recipe is really a hot salad, it is included with the salads. It can also be served as a side dish or entree, one you will find delicious.

*Naomi*

# Marie McCaw Stanley's
# Baked Dungeness Crab Salad  1950s

We who live in the Pacific Northwest know we are blessed with an abundance of fresh seafood year round. Dungeness crab is surely the favorite of natives and visitors alike.

½ - ¾ pound fresh Dungeness crab meat

1 cup fresh red pepper, cut in ¼-inch cubes

¼ cup chopped celery

¼ cup chopped onion

1 cup Best Foods mayonnaise

4 hard boiled eggs, cut in quarters, then in thirds

1 Tablespoon Worchestershire sauce

Mix, adding eggs last. Spoon into flat baking dish and top with cracker crumbs. Dot with butter. Bake at 350 degrees 30-40 minutes.

*Naomi*

# Dungeness Crab Louie   1950s

In San Francisco in the early 1950s I discovered Crab Louie in a charming restaurant in Maiden Lane. When I arrived home, I found I could create the same marvelous salad. Always a special treat on a warm day, it is colorful and truly offers a taste of summer.

If you are adventuresome you may crack and prepare crab for this wonderful salad. I prefer to bring home the fresh crabmeat ready to use.

Four Crab Louies:

    2 fresh Dungeness crabs

    1 head iceberg lettuce, finely sliced

    1 small green pepper, seeded and cut in ¼-inch rings

    4 green onions, cut in ¼-inch pieces

    1 avocado, cut in thin slices

    2 small tomatoes, cut in wedges

    2 small jars marinated artichoke hearts, well drained
        and cut in quarters if large

    12 small whole asparagus spears, either canned or fresh,
        steamed, and chilled

Dressing:

    1 cup Best Foods mayonnaise

    1-2 Tablespoons fresh lemon juice

    4 Tablespoons catsup

    1-2 Tablespoons horseradish

    2 teaspoons Johnny's Salad Elegance, if available (seasoning salt is okay)

    freshly ground black pepper

Line dinner plates with outer lettuce leaves. Mound shredded lettuce in center and place 3 pepper rings, 3 avocado slices, 3 tomato wedges and 3 artichoke hearts at the base of lettuce mound. Add green onions to top of lettuce, then crab. Add 3 asparagus spears, tepee style, to each salad. Spoon dressing over crab and serve with hot dinner rolls.

Note: Johnny's Salad Elegance is a special seasoning mixture that is wonderful on barbecued salmon and toasted sourdough french bread or in salad dressings and sauces for fish. Made by Johnny's Enterprises, Tacoma, Washington.

*Naomi*

*About 1901. Great Uncle Sam Erwin was the perfect Uncle Sam in the 4th of July pageant at Prescott. Cousins Ruth and Jay McCaw portrayed Martha and George Washington. A grand picnic was enjoyed by the entire community.*

# Grandmother Ida McCaw's
# Cream Soup   1890s

Take one quart chicken broth, strain, add one cup rich, sweet milk and season to suit the taste with salt and pepper. Diced chicken can be added for a heartier soup.

*Ruth McCaw Merrill*

# Grandmother Emma McCaw's
# Family Potato Soup   1920s

Large dinner bells were found on most of the ranches but at Grandfather Robert and Emma McCaw's home they used a large Conch shell that would be blown by Grandmother Emma to call the men to dinner from their work in the fields. This heirloom is still in their family, owned by a grandson.

   4 potatoes, diced
   2 onions
   2 stalks celery, diced
   1  teaspoon salt
   Whole milk or cream

Cook in water until soft. Drain off water. Add milk or cream. Salt and pepper to taste. Serve very hot.

Note: Grandmother Emma added homemade noodles to this delicious winter soup. Lois adds chopped parsley. Bacon can also be added.

*Lois McCaw Ellsaesser*

# Ruth McCaw Merrill's
## Tomato Soup   1920s

Tomato and potato soup were favorites long ago. This one is a reminder of Grandmother's cooking.

Take one large can of tomatoes and when boiling add ½ teaspoon soda
and stir till froth disappears then strain or not as liked. Set back on stove
and when hot add ½ cup fine cracker crumbs, pinch of salt, 2 Tablespoons butter and some pepper. Lastly add a pint of boiling whole milk,
serve at once.

Note: Italian-style seasoned tomatoes are wonderful, adding a little zip to the soup. Put tomatoes into blender or chop finely. Bring milk just to the boiling point over medium heat. This is wonderful with homemade bread fresh and hot from the oven.

*Kay and Dennis Stanley*

# European
# Tomato Gin Soup   1980s

Several years ago when we were traveling in Europe we enjoyed this wonderful soup in a charming hotel dining room. Banks of fresh flowers created a beautiful setting as the soup was prepared in a chafing dish at our table. We believe it to be the best soup ever! It should be created only in summer and early fall when tomatoes are available right from the garden.

Tomato basis:

      4 large beefsteak tomatoes

      1 large can peeled tomatoes

      Salt, pepper, and fresh basil to taste

Cut fresh and canned tomatoes in quarters. Place in heavy saucepan and cook over medium or medium-low heat until reduced to 1½ quarts. Stir often with flat-ended cooking spoon to prevent sticking. With a wooden spoon, run tomatoes through a sieve. Remove ½ cup and cool in small saucepan. Sprinkle 3 envelopes Knox plain gelatin over surface. Shake gently to mix. Let set 1 minute, then place over medium heat, stirring constantly until gelatin is dissolved. Slowly add 1 cup hot juice, then return to rest of juice. Remove from heat and pour into gelatin molds, cool and refrigerate.

Preparation of the soup (at the table) for two portions:

      Soften 4 Tablespoons butter and add ½ shallot, cut in very thin slices; 1 small mushroom, thinly sliced; and several fresh basil leaves, cut in strips.

In a chafing dish:

      Place butter mixture and heat gently until mushrooms begin to change color. Add 4 Tablespoons warm gin and heat for about 1 minute. Add tomato mold and heat to simmer. Pour 3 Tablespoons whipping cream into bowls, add soup and garnish with strips of fresh basil. Served with crusty sourdough french bread, this different and fragrant soup will please your family and guests.

*Naomi*

# John Sawyer's
# Après Ski Ham *&* Bean Soup  1990s

At their cabin on Lake Wenatchee in Washington's Cascade Mountains, Pat and John welcome family and friends after a day of skiing with this savory soup.

First Part:

     1 ham bone with meat or several smoked pork shanks

     1¼ cups mixed beans, soaked overnight

     3 cups water

     1 cup chicken broth

Cover and simmer 2 hours.

Second Part:

     2 cups water

     1 medium onion, chopped

     1 14-ounce can peeled chopped tomatoes

     1 cup chopped carrots

     2 stalks celery

     ¼ cup lemon juice

     ¼ teaspoon red pepper flakes

Remove ham bone, shredding meat and removing all fat. Add above ingredients and simmer 1-1½ hours and serve piping hot. Individual round sourdough loaves make interesting and delicious soup bowls. Cut off the tops and remove bread inside, leaving one inch of bread and crust on the outside. Place on cookie sheet and toast lightly in a 350 degree oven for several minutes.

Note: Smoked turkey wings are another choice for the meat. They are delicious, taste just like ham and have less salt. Choose any combination of dried beans such as small red, baby lima, navy, black, kidney, pinto, and large lima and combine in the proportions you prefer. Divide into several plastic bags for future use.

*Pat and John Sawyer*

*Direct descendents of William and Sarah McCaw. Photograph taken June 28, 1986 at Prescott High School Reunion. Left to right: (front row) Kathleen McCaw Bergevin, Alene Vernon Bedford, Lois McCaw Ellsaesser, Dorothy Vernon Avril, Naomi Stanley Martin Kulp, Jesse Stanley, Ruth McCaw Merrill, Carolyn McCaw Houger, Elizabeth Merrill, Bob McCaw, Jean Erwin Ronald. Back row: Sam Erwin, Dennis Stanley, Jim Erwin, Katie Erwin Oliver, Marilyn McCaw Griffin, Norman Stanley, Martin McCaw, Steve Erwin, Terry Bedford, Scott Erwin, and Kenneth McCaw.*

# Wheat Berry
# Chicken Soup   1990s

Although we produced millions of bushels of wheat on our ranches, I don't believe our grandmothers and mothers cooked with the wheat, except for breakfast cereal and breads.

Just a year ago I discovered this marvelous wheat for cooking many interesting dishes and developed this recipe. When cooked the wheat is chewy, a bit crunchy, and delicious. It is a plentiful resource that could have been used many years ago. Soft white wheat is the best for soup, chili, and stew. It can be added to almost any baking recipe. It is surprisingly delicious in hearty chicken or beef soup. After trying wheat you may never again cook with barley! Wheat kernels are now known as wheat berries, an intriguing name for a very important grain.

1 large roasting or stewing hen

2 cups dry "white wheat" berries

1 large onion

2 large stalks celery

2 large carrots

1 medium potato

1 turnip

¼ small head cabbage

1-2 cans tomatoes

2 Tablespoons Soy Sauce, adding more later (to taste)

2-3 garlic cloves

1 Tablespoon Chicken bouillon, adding more if desired

Basil, thyme, bay leaves

Pasta—small corkscrews or wheels

Measure and rinse the wheat, then soak overnight with lots of water. The next morning place the chicken in a large kettle and cover with water. Add chopped onion and sliced celery with green tops. Add soy sauce and chicken bouillon with desired spices and cook over medium heat. Add drained wheat when the chicken is about half done. Remove chicken when done, cool to lukewarm and remove meat from bones and cut in bite sized pieces. Return chicken to soup kettle. About an hour before serving add the chopped or sliced vegetables and tomatoes, and 15- 20 minutes before serving add the pasta and taste the broth, adding more of any flavoring you wish. Stir once in a while. Soy sauce is the secret ingredient and gives a rich, satisfying flavor to the soup.

Note: White wheat can be found in natural food stores and specialty food markets. It is inexpensive and an exciting new grain to try. The soaked wheat berries can be frozen for cooking at a later time. The pasta can be cooked separately and added to the soup just before serving so it won't be overdone.

*Naomi*

# Grandmother Emma McCaw & Ethel McCaw Vernon's Boston Baked Beans   1880s

Mother baked the beans in a big roaster pan covered with an ironstone plate. Since the pan was red hot, coming from the wood stove in our home in the Touchet Valley near Prescott, she always tied a big flour sack dish towel around it and we carried it to the picnic holding onto the top knot. The beans always tasted even better cold the next day.

    2 cups small navy beans
    ½ pound lean salt pork
    1 teaspoon salt
    ¾ teaspoon prepared mustard, optional
    1 cup tomatoes
    1 large dry onion
    1 cup brown sugar

Soak beans in cold water (to cover, overnight or all day while you are at school or work). Drain off cold water and add hot water to cover beans, let simmer with a little soda (about ½ teaspoon) for ten minutes.

Drain the beans and cover again with hot water. Cook slowly about 1½ hours. Cut the salt pork in one inch pieces and add to the beans while this cooking is going on. Now add the tomatoes, brown sugar, onion slices, salt, and mustard.

Pour into a casserole (or any pan) and bake slowly for about three hours. Cook in oven with a lid (or old plate) over the beans. Remove cover the last half hour to brown the beans. Watch carefully all the time and do not let the beans become too dry. You can keep adding tomato juice or water. Sample the beans when they are baking, as you might want to add more sugar or salt.

Dorothy's Note: As I was going on a ski trip next day, Mother added, "Cook the night before you plan to leave—keep in ice box until the next day. Good luck!"

*Dorothy Vernon Avril*

# The
# Asparagus Patch

Grandfather Edwin planted a large asparagus field of several acres across the road from our house, by the large orchard. In asparagus season we would walk over and cut enough for dinner or supper that evening. It would be cooked within a few minutes of cutting and was the most delicious treat.

One fall Grandfather didn't mound the rows of asparagus in his large field. Mounding the rows produced white asparagus that hadn't yet emerged from the soil. That next spring he cut boxes of green asparagus and took it by wagon to the grocer in Prescott, where he had been selling white asparagus for years. The grocer looked at the color and refused to buy it, saying that his customers would never consider eating green asparagus! Grandfather then drove around to friends and neighbors who were delighted to try it. They thought it was delicious. Later in the day the grocer drove several miles to find Grandfather and told him that he would buy this new green asparagus. Too late, Grandfather said, for he had found a new, enthusiastic market that wanted all he could produce, and at a higher price!

# Marie McCaw Stanley's
# Sweet Sour Cabbage   1920s

When you prepare cabbage in this way, you can create a hot dish with an unusual, wonderfully tart and tangy flavor. A family favorite shared by Bessie, Ruth, and Marie, from their mother, Ida.

Cut four or five slices of very lean bacon into small strips about ¼-⅜ inch wide, cook, and drain. Dice or finely shred cabbage to make 4 to 6 cups. Put in large kettle of boiling water and stir from bottom. Let stand 2 minutes. Put in strainer and cover to keep hot. Mix together 2 beaten eggs, ½ cup sugar, ½ cup cider vinegar, ½ teaspoon salt. Add bacon to above egg mixture and pour into hot cabbage which has been put back into pan. Heat on medium and simmer for 2 minutes until hot and bubbly. Serve at once.

*Naomi*

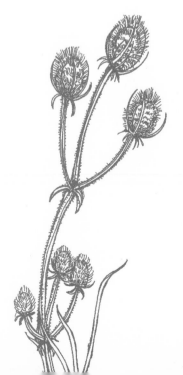

70

# Cream of the Crop
## Dried Corn   1920s

Sweet corn, sometimes many acres, was grown for the family and the harvest crew. In addition to serving it fresh, the women dried the corn for winter. The rich flavor and creaminess of this dish added an interesting taste and texture to winter fare.

Cut fresh corn from cob and scrape well. To each 8 pints of corn add ½ cup sugar, ¼ cup salt, and ½ cup cream. Stir together in shallow pan and cook for 20 minutes. Stir constantly after it starts to boil to prevent burning. Dry by your preferred method. It requires only a small amount of water and a short cooking period to be ready for use. When cooked, season with salt, pepper, and cream.

Note: Corn was dried by spreading kernels on a screen placed on boxes or sawhorses. Covered with cheesecloth, it would dry in the sun. Then it would be stored in jars or tins for winter use.

*Prescott Home Economics Club Cookbook, 1942*

# Bessie McCaw Shupe's
## Harvest Time Onions   1930s

Take off the tops and tails, and the thin outer skin, lest the onions should go to pieces. Lay them on the bottom of a pan which is broad enough to contain them without piling one on another. Just cover them with water, and let them simmer slowly until they are tender all through, but not till they break.

Some cooks use two waters in cooking onions. By pouring off the first water and adding more, the strong taste is destroyed. Serve with melted butter and milk, thickened to a cream with a small amount of flour.

An excellent way to handle onions without crying is to fill a pan with water and hold and peel each onion under the water.

*Connie Plants and Mary Shupe McCarthy*

72

*1915. An unusual balancing act at Grandfather Stanley's farm.*

73

## Crispy Potato Patties
## with Boysenberry Syrup   1950s

Grate several large potatoes. Melt about 2 Tablespoons butter and 2 Tablespoons Crisco vegetable shortening in a large, heavy frying pan.

Take a small handful of grated potatoes and add to the melted shortening. Flatten with a pancake turner. Repeat until the bottom of the pan is covered, usually three or four patties. Salt lightly. Cook until golden and crispy, then turn over and cook the other side. Drain on paper towels and serve very hot with cold raspberry or boysenberry syrup. These are a special treat for breakfast or supper.

## Raspberry  or Boysenberry Syrup   1950s

Boil 4 cups berries with 2 Tablespoons lemon juice for 2 minutes in a large, heavy pan. Add 4 cups sugar and boil on medium high for 3-4 minutes. Pour into large sieve over glass or stainless bowl and stir with wooden spoon until juice is removed. Scrape outside of sieve with rubber spatula. Pour hot syrup into quart jar and seal or into freezer container. Keeps very well in refrigerator and can be frozen.

For preserves, boil berries for 5 minutes and seal in small jars.

*Naomi*

# Golden Apple Slices   1960s

Peel and core several yellow delicious apples. In a frying pan, place 2 Tablespoons butter. When melted add the sliced apples and cover. Cook over medium heat about 5 minutes until done. Turn apples at least once. Apples will be shiny and almost transparent. Serve with pork, or other meat.

*Naomi*

# Libby McCaw's
# Apple Filled Pumpkin   1980s

Find a nice, fat, round, small to medium-sized pumpkin and clean out the inside and the lid. To fill the pumpkin, peel and slice Yellow Delicious or other apple that holds its shape when cooked. Gently mix with 2 teaspoons cinnamon, 3-4 Tablespoons brown sugar, 2-3 Tablespoons butter or margarine, and ½-¾ cup raisins. Fill pumpkin, replace lid, and put in a heavy cast iron dutch oven or baking pan (with 4-inch sides). Bake in the oven at 350 degrees for about one hour, or until pumpkin looks cooked but still holds its shape. You can peek inside to check the apples for doneness. Serve from the pumpkin, scraping some of the pumpkin with the apples. This is colorful and fun to serve for a potluck dinner or special occasion.

*Libby McCaw*

# Shivaree

Ingredients:
1 Bride
1 Bridegroom
1 Night, dark or semi-dark
Pots, pans, bells, gongs, etc.
50 or so noisy neighbors

Sprinkle neighbors liberally but secretly around house of newly married couple. At signal, activate pots, pans, bells, and gongs. Lace vigorously with shouts, yells, whistles, etc. Continue until very hot. Couple will emerge from house bright red with embarrassment.

Warning: The Shivaree crowd should be at least as smart as the shivareed, or things could get too hot.

When Ernest and Lilla McCaw were married in 1929, the large crowd of neighbors crept stealthily into the big grove of locust trees in their front yard and let go. After a lengthy and raucous serenade, the celebrants stopped the music, but two of their number continued beating on their pots, yelling loudly. When the ringleaders tried to discover which culprits had such poor taste, they found Lilla and Earnest, the bride and bridegroom, happily banging away and not one bit embarrassed.

*Written by Paul McCaw*

# Grandmother Amanda McCaw Erwin's
## Tomato Catsup   1880s

If you have an overabundance of tomatoes in your garden and you'd like to experiment with an old, old recipe, this would be fun to try. It was not tested but it does sound interesting.

One bushel ripe tomatoes, wipe with a clean cloth, cut up into a granite kettle, put on to cook with one quart water, boil until tomatoes are tender then run through colander. Return to kettle, add one-half gallon strong vinegar, let boil until thick, then add one ounce mixed spice, one ounce cloves, one ounce black pepper, two nutmegs, grated, two pounds brown sugar, and one scant cup salt. Bottle and seal.

Note: The granite kettle was one of the old type made of ironware with a surface of grayish or bluish mottled enamel.

*Ladies of the Presbyterian Church Cookbook, Prescott, 1903*

# Grandmother Holling's
## Cream Cheese   1920s

With an abundance of fresh milk and cream our grandmothers and mothers often made cream and cottage cheese to use the milk.

Mix thoroughly 1 quart firm curds, 1 cup butter, 1½ teaspoons baking soda and 1½ teaspoons salt. Let stand two hours. Place in double boiler and stir until melted. Add 1 cup thick cream, sweet or sour, and cook 30 minutes or until smooth, then pour into mold. Pimiento added when cool is good.

*Mae Temple McCaw's recipe via Ruth McCaw (Mrs. Robert H.)*

# Amanda McCaw Erwin's
## Dill Pickles   1920s

Fill jars with washed cucumbers. Pack jars full and add ½ teaspoon mustard seed and ½ cup dill. Add 1 clove garlic if desired. Heat to boiling point 1 cup salt, 1 quart vinegar and 3 quarts water. Pour over cucumbers and seal.

*Della Mae Erwin Sanders*

# Aunt Margaret Erwin's
## Pickles   1930s

Dennis Stanley recently recalled a vignette, familiar to all the women in our Prescott area. Until the 1940s or later the Watkins man would arrive every few months at each ranch and farm with his treasury of wonderful spices made by the Watkins Company in Minnesota. In the early 1900s he covered the miles with his horse and wagon, his large box of spices under the seat. In later years he drove a black truck that was his home on the road. He was always warmly welcomed by the women in the family, who enjoyed a good visit while carefully selecting their spices for the coming months. If he arrived around mealtime he was usually invited to join the family. The Watkins man brought the freshest and best spices available anywhere, including real vanilla, fresh whole nutmeg, pepper, and the kinds of spices needed for the wonderful pickles we made.

    3 cups sugar
    1 cup cider vinegar
    2 Tablespoons whole allspice
    Dash of garlic salt
    Medium sized cucumbers, cut in thirds

Wash the cucumbers and put in jars. Boil the sugar, vinegar and garlic salt 5 minutes. Remove from heat and add allspice. Pour over cucumbers and refrigerate for about a week before using.

*Mae Jean Williams*

# Marie McCaw Stanley's
## Spiced Peaches & Pears   1930s

At our holiday dinners we always enjoyed mother's spiced peaches and pears. They were made as soon as we picked the fruit and were kept in the cool cellar until Thanksgiving and Christmas. They are wonderful with ham.

For 2 quarts:

> 6-7 small whole canning peaches or Bartlett pears
>
> 3 cups good cider vinegar
>
> 6½ cups sugar
>
> 2 Tablespoons whole cloves

Remove skins from peaches by placing in a sieve and dipping into boiling water about 10 seconds, then cooling in ice water. The skins will easily slip off. Boil sugar, water and cloves 5 minutes to make syrup. Add peaches or pears and boil over medium heat 7-8 minutes, just until tender when pricked with a fork. With a large spoon place fruit in sterilized jars, add syrup, wipe rim of jar with a cloth dipped into boiling water, and seal. Do not pack tightly. Store in a cool, dark place until Thanksgiving when they will be ready to chill and serve for your holiday dinner.

*Naomi*

# Grandmother's Day

Grandmother, on a winter's day
Milked the cows, and fed them hay
Slopped the hogs, saddled the mule
And got the children off to School.....

Did a washing, mopped the floors
Washed the windows and did some chores
Cooked a dish of home-dried fruit
And pressed her husband's Sunday suit.....

Swept the parlor, made the beds
Baked a dozen loaves of bread
Split some fire-wood and lugged in
Enough to fill the kitchen bin.....

Cleaned the lamps and put in oil
Stewed some apples she thought would spoil
Churned the butter and baked a cake
Then exclaimed, "For Heaven's Sake"....

The calfs have got out of the pen
Went out and chased them in again
Gathered the eggs and locked the stable
Back to the house to set the table.....

Cooked a supper that was delicious
And afterwards washed up all the dishes
Fed the cat and sprinkled the clothes
And mended a basketful of hose.....

Then she opened the organ and began to play,
"When you come to the end of a PERFECT DAY".....

*Author Unknown, Contributed by Connie Shupe Plants*

*1930s. Thirty eight mules worked hard to pull the combine on the steep hills of the skyrocket near Prescott. Each man on the crew was assigned six to eight mules to feed, water and harness in the early morning. Two hours at noontime gave the mules time to eat and rest. Dennis and Norman Stanley worked as teenagers on the combine. Dennis operated the header to cut the wheat at the correct height. The cut grain then moved by belt to the separator and was blown through a double spout into burlap sacks. Jigged up and down to settle the wheat, they were quickly sewn and put onto the chute on the side of the combine. Soon released in groups of five, they were later picked up by team and wagon.*

# Marie McCaw Stanley's
## Sunshine Strawberry Jam   1940s

Uncle Ernest made certain that he had a large strawberry patch with his favorite berry called Redheart. The berries did have bright red color to the very heart and were sweet and juicy, the best taste of spring. As soon as lots of berries were picked, we hurried home to make this delightful jam.

Place 1 quart of berries and 2 cups sugar in a kettle. Bring to a quick boil, stirring just enough to dissolve the sugar. As soon as the mixture is boiling, add 2 more cups of sugar and boil briskly for 10 minutes. Add 2 Tablespoons cider vinegar and remove from fire. Pour into an open container and let stand 24-48 hours or until thickened. Seal cold with parafin in jelly jars.

*Kay and Dennis Stanley*

# Norine's Old Fashioned
# Mustard Pickles   1920s

Norine Paton is a charming, dear little lady of 92, the mother of my special friend Pat Sawyer. Norine lives in Cashmere, Washington, and is still active. Her comment regarding pickle making: "Cucumbers grow so fast, for just the right size you really should pick them in the middle of the night!"

When August arrives and you want to make some special pickles, try this old recipe.

24 small cucumbers, sliced into ½-inch rounds

2 quarts small white onions, peeled

2 small heads cauliflower, cut in small chunks

3 green peppers, cut into small strips

2 quarts sliced green tomatoes

Put one cup of salt in enough water to cover ingredients and let stand overnight. In the morning, scald in the same water 10-15 minutes but do not boil. Drain.

Mix:

4 cups sugar

2 Tablespoons celery seed

¾ cup flour

2 ounces ground mustard

½ ounce ground turmeric

Add 3 quarts cider vinegar and vegetables and bring to a boil. Put in hot scalded jars to seal. Let set in a cool pantry for one month. Serve to your family and guests with pride, giving them a taste of pickles from grandmother and great grandmother's day.

*Naomi*

# Summer Garden
## Sweet Pickle Chunks   1960s

This is one of those very special recipes. It is so popular with our family and friends that I'm now making 20-30 quarts at a time. This old recipe came originally from a magazine, decades ago. With a few changes I have made, I hope it will win a place in your treasury of special recipes.

12 medium pickling cucumbers, 5 inches long and 1½ inches in diameter

8 cups sugar

3 Tablespoons Schilling Mixed Pickling Spices

5 teaspoons pickling salt

4 cups apple cider vinegar

⅛ teaspoon powdered alum

Make pickles as soon as possible after picking cucumbers. Gently scrub each one and remove a thin slice from the blossom end. Prick 2 times with a table fork. Place cucumbers in an enamel canning kettle. Cover with boiling water. Do not put lid on kettle. Let stand until the next morning. Drain and repeat this procedure the next three mornings. On the fifth day, drain and slice the cucumbers crosswise into chunks about ¾-1 inch long. Combine the vinegar, salt and spices and bring to boiling. Pour over cucumbers. Let stand two days. On the third day, bring just to a simmer, add alum, stir, and seal in hot, sterilized wide-mouth jars.

Note: Pickles are usually made in August and September. I always make at least 6 recipes at one time, putting 3 recipes of cucumbers in one canning kettle and 3 in another. For the best flavor, buy new spices each year. Let pickles stand in a cool, dark place until Thanksgiving when they are ready to enjoy.

Best served icy cold. Crisp and crunchy, they are marvelous!

*Naomi*

# Harvesting

Wheat harvesting usually began around the Fourth of July and ended about Labor Day. This remarkable scene was captured between 1910 and 1915 at the Edwin McCaw ranch near Prescott by a traveling photographer who visited many of the ranches and farms in our area.

Recently Dennis Stanley explained the harvesting procedure. The standing wheat was cut by several headers that were pushed by the team of horses or mules. This prevented trampling of the grain. The cut wheat fell onto the draper, a moving belt of canvas with hickory sticks, and moved upward to fall into the header box, actually a large wagon with one side higher than the other to compensate for the sloping hills. When the header was filled, it would be driven to the derrick. Each header box had a canvas liner that was picked up by the derrick .

Several men would pitch the wheat into the thresher to separate the grains from the straw. The most interesting and important part of this operation was the big steam engine. Fed by straw or wood it ran the belt that operated the threshing machine. The belt was usually very long for two reasons. First, it allowed the engine to remain a safe distance from the thresher, preventing fires. Second, the long distance was required to keep the huge belt from sliding off the drive wheel of the thresher.

In those days, wagon loads of water were required to keep the thresher running and sometimes it threatened to run dry. When that happened, shrill blasts on the steam whistle signaled the water tank drivers to hurry with their loads, sometimes calling them to bring their cigar-shaped tanks from miles away.

The cow tied to the old car in the lower left-hand corner of the scene below gave a welcome supply of rich milk for coffee breaks.

*From the collection of E. R. McCaw*

# Main Dishes & Sauces

## Main Dishes

## Sauces

*1916-19. Left to right, sisters Marie, Ruth, and Bessie McCaw returned home from Oregon State College and cooked for the harvest crew in a wooden cookhouse on skids that had been pulled by a team of horses or mules to a location near the harvesters. During the harvest the women would arise as early as 4:30 a.m. to cook a large breakfast for fifteen to eighteen men. Dinner was served at noon and included meat, vegetables, fruit, hot bread, cakes, and pies. Supper was similar to the noontime meal. Baking took several hours each day when the outside temperatures sometimes reached 110 degrees in the shade.*

# Grandmother Ida McCaw's
## Beefsteak Roll   1890s

Each ranch in our valley had a large cast iron dinner bell on a tall pole by the kitchen door. The rope hanging down was always a temptation to the children, but we were discouraged from ringing it because it had several important uses. Besides being rung before every meal to bring the men in from the fields, it was used to bring help in case of fire or other emergency. Ordinarily, though, the bell called hungry folks home for some of their favorite meals—like Grandmother Ida's beefsteak roll.

Grandma's Recipe:

> Remove the bone from a slice of round steak. Make a stuffing of one cup of stale bread crumbs, one Tablespoonful butter, a teaspoonful of salt, one quarter teaspoonful of sage or half teaspoonful of thyme, or both. Moisten with hot water. Season the steak with salt and pepper and spread the stuffing on it. Roll up and tie or skewer to keep the stuffing in. Put some bacon drippings in a frying pan. Dredge steak with flour and brown on all sides. Put in a baking pan or crock (casserole dish) and cover the roll with boiling water. Put a tight cover on the dish and bake in a moderate oven for two hours. Turn over when half done. Thicken the gravy and serve with the meat.

Kay's Update:

> Use a baking pan not much larger than the roll and cover only half the roll with water. We liked the boiled beef flavor with horse radish. Adding 1 teaspoon sage and 1 teaspoon thyme gives more flavor.

*Kay and Dennis Stanley*

# Grandmother Ida McCaw's
## Meat Pie   1890s

Each Sunday Grandfather Edwin, Grandmother Ida and their children rode in their buggy two and one half miles to the Presbyterian Church in Prescott. Over Grandmother's objections, Grandfather took along several of his sheep dogs. Along the way he would stop the buggy, perhaps several times, to discipline a wayward dog. When they finally reached Prescott, Grandmother was very annoyed, for they nearly always walked into church late, interrupting the service while seating the family. Grandfather had some explaining to do! Afterwards, when his transgression was forgotten, he often enjoyed his wife's meat pie for Sunday dinners.

Take light bread dough and line baking pan. Add cooked chicken,
lamb, or beef chunks and put on cover (top crust). Let rise as you
do bread. When ready to bake, add the gravy through openings in
top of pie. Bake at 350 degrees for 30-45 minutes.

*Kay and Dennis Stanley*

# Grandmother Emma's
## Chicken Tamale Pie a la McCaw   1910s

Slowly simmer a nice fat chicken in boiling water to cover until very, very tender, adding salt to taste and a large chopped onion, as it cooks. Let chicken remain in broth until cold, then carefully pick from the bones. Take two cups of yellow corn meal and moisten in cold water, then stir into briskly boiling broth. Stir a few minutes, cover, and reduce heat to a simmer for ½ hour. If more mush is wanted, add some water and use more corn meal, but do not have cereal too thick as it stiffens when cold. Butter a large baking pan or casserole, line with cornmeal. Cover this with bite size pieces of chicken, add green or stuffed olives, then cover with either of the prepared sauces and fill pan with cornmeal. Cover and store in refrigerator until needed. To serve, heat thoroughly in hot oven, about 400 degrees. Pass additional hot sauce if desired.

First Sauce:

Moisten till smooth one large Tablespoon chili powder in a kettle. To moisten use part cold water and part olive liquid. Add 2 cans Giblet gravy, ½ cube (or a little more) butter, and a dash each of salt, garlic, and onion salt. Place on heat and stir until hot, then let mixture stand a little while to blend. Some sauce is excellent to pass. This can be seasoned for hotter sauce for those who like it.

Second Sauce:

Moisten chili powder as above, then add 2 cups water. Bring to a boil, thicken as desired and cook well. Add butter and three types of salt. This is also very good in the tamale pie and as sauce, but double recipe if using in both places.

*Jerrianne Powell*

# Ada Williams'
# Baked Ham  1920s

One 12-pound uncooked ham. Skin and stick the fat side with whole cloves. In a pan place 1 cup honey, 1 Tablespoon dry mustard, ½ teaspoon cloves, ½ teaspoon allspice, 2 bay leaves. Mix with 1¼ cups flour until stiff enough to roll out on bread board. Roll out and cover the ham, placed in a heavy cast iron skillet. Bake 7 hours. Bake 2 hours at 350 degrees then reduce heat to 300 degrees. Do not add any water. Ham has a unique covering, similar to a crust but puffy and flavorful.

*Prescott Home Economics Club Cookbook, 1942*

# Bessie McCaw Shupe and Ida McCaw's
## Eggs a la Goldenrod   1920s

In the 1800s when a young woman came to cook for our Great Aunt Mary she told Mary she was a fine, experienced cook. The next morning Aunt Mary requested soft boiled eggs for breakfast. After waiting and waiting at the table she called to the girl, who rushed in with a most unhappy look. She was almost in tears when she cried out, "Miz Erwin, I've been boiling and boiling those eggs for just the longest time and they won't ever get soft!"

6 Tablespoons butter

6 Tablespoons flour

1 teaspoon salt

⅛ teaspoon hot pepper sauce

9 hard boiled eggs

3 cups milk

First boil the eggs in simmering water for 10 minutes. Rinse under cold water and remove shells. Make a white sauce of the butter, flour, and milk. Add salt. Cook slowly on medium until thickened, then add hot pepper sauce after removing from heat.

Reserve 3 egg yolks; coarsely chop whites of these three eggs. Quarter remaining 6 eggs, add to white sauce with chopped whites. Pour over lightly toasted white bread or in Patty Shells. Sieve the egg yolks over the top. Serves 6.

*Mary Shupe McCarthy*

# Katherine Holling McCaw's
# Harvest Hash   1920s

When this hearty dish was prepared during wheat harvest, it was doubled and tripled to feed 12 to 18 hungry men.

Dice up 2 raw potatoes. Place in a large oven-proof skillet, salt, and pour on 1 cup of water. Cover skillet and cook on top of stove until potatoes are tender. Grind up a large onion and cooked meat (left over roast beef is preferred). Grind in that order so that the meat will clean the onion odor out of the grinder. Add onion, meat, and pepper to the potatoes. Cover skillet and place in 350 degree oven for 30 minutes. Uncover skillet and bake 15 minutes longer.

*Kathleen McCaw Bergevin*

# Paul McCaw's Vignettes

## Watermelon

Water + Melon; from its abundant watery juice. A large round or oblong fruit with a hard green rind and a juicy pink or red pulp containing many seeds. A frivolous melon; it is not a serious melon as is the Casaba or Persian. It is for this reason that a culture not given to thievery condones the stealing of watermelons in the patch. In fact, studies have shown that watermelon tastes significantly better when stolen from the patch. In 1913 at the High School in Prescott, Washington, a small wheat farming community near the Blue Mountains, Ernest McCaw faced an ethical dilemma when his classmates urged him to join them in a watermelon raid. Not wishing to participate in theft, Ernest took charge of the expedition and led the dozen High School boys into the wheat hills, winding a circuitous route through the canyons in the moonlight, coming upon a large watermelon patch in the summer fallow, where they feasted in ecstasy. None of the boys ever knew that Ernest had led them to his McCaw family's own watermelon patch.

## Summer Fallow

The secret of raising wheat in a dry climate is to use two years moisture for one year's crop. This is done by letting the land lie fallow (plowed, with a thin mulch on top) for one year. The McCaw family of Prescott always planted a large patch of melons several acres in size, in the summer fallow, spacing them far apart on the North hillside where there was more moisture. An extra big patch was needed, as the harvest crews were large and the work was hot. In addition, teen age boys thought it great sport to steal watermelons and there were coyotes who thought so too.

# Marie McCaw Stanley's
## Savory Chicken and Dumplings   1920s

For chicken and dumplings, mother added to the broth the cluster of small eggs found inside the hen and, I believe, at least one beaten egg yolk. The liquid was rich and always a creamy yellow in color. The richness and color also came from the chickens running free on the ranch and eating lots of green grass. The oldest chickens made the richest broth.

Cook the chicken in a large stewpot covered with water. Add 1 large stalk celery, sliced, and 1 onion, chopped. Add 1-2 Tablespoons soy sauce and 2-3 bouillon cubes, adding more when chicken is cooked, if desired.

Dumplings:
  2 cups sifted flour
  4 teaspoons baking powder
  1 teaspoon salt
  1 cup milk
  4 Tablespoons salad oil

Sift dry ingredients together. Add liquids and stir just enough to mix. Drop by Tablespoonful into boiling broth and onto the chicken. Place lid on kettle and cook over medium heat 12-15 minutes without lifting the lid. No peeking! This amount will serve a family of four.

Note: To update this recipe for today's busy cooks try Jiffy Biscuit Mix, using the recipe on the box. Try adding the soy sauce for richness and flavor.

*Naomi*

# Marie McCaw Stanley's
# Creamed Tuna on Crackers   1920s

This recipe and the one that follows are two light dishes that are easy to prepare and tasty for lunch or dinner. Children enjoy them too.

Melt 4 Tablespoons butter in a heavy saucepan. Add 4 Tablespoons flour and blend. Add 1½ cups regular milk. Over medium heat, stir while cooking until thickened. Drain 2 cans light meat tuna, packed in oil, then break up a bit with a dinner fork. Add to white sauce and heat on low until mixture is bubbling. Cook gently 2-3 minutes. Add a little pepper. Serve over saltine crackers on individual dinner plates.

# Marie McCaw Stanley's
# Chipped Beef on Crackers   1920s

Use the same recipe for the white sauce as for the Creamed Tuna. Add one 4- or 6-ounce package or jar of dried chipped beef that you have soaked in warm water for about 20 seconds, then snipped into pieces about 1 x 1½ inches before adding to the white sauce. Briefly soaking the dried beef in water removes some of the salt. Drain on paper towel before adding to white sauce.

*Naomi*

# Lilla McCaw's
## Ranch Tuna Pie   1930s

2 medium carrots, diced and cooked

1 small onion, chopped, cooked two minutes in butter

3 Tablespoons butter

1 teaspoon salt

⅛ teaspoon pepper

½ teaspoon paprika

2 cans tuna

2 small potatoes, ½ inch diced and cooked five minutes

2 cups peas

1 cup grated sharp cheddar

White sauce:

3 Tablespoons butter

3 Tablespoons flour

1¾ cups milk

Make a pastry for the top. Combine all ingredients and place in a shallow baking dish. Make white sauce and put it in last of all. Add crust to the top and sprinkle cheese over top. Cut a center hole in crust about 2 inches in diameter and several slits. Bake in the oven at 375 degrees for about 30-40 minutes until crust is nicely browned and casserole is bubbly in the center.

Note: If frozen peas are used, thaw and bring to room temperature before adding. The casserole is done when it is bubbling in the center and the crust is golden brown.

*Paul McCaw, Carolyn McCaw Houger, Marilyn McCaw Griffin*

*When harvesting in the 1920s and 1930s, Grandfather Edwin used a combine that was pulled by thirty-eight mules. The mule skinner was seated at the end of a slanting ladder out over the mules, which were placed in the team according to their dispositions and abilities. Many of the rounded hills were very steep, requiring patience and skill by the mule skinner and the mules!*

# Margaret Erwin's
## Smoked Beef & Macaroni   1930s

Aunt Margaret's version: "I like to make my own macaroni and cheese. I moisten it to the consistency we like with a can of mushroom soup and season it with minced onion and Worchestershire sauce. I like it because the ingredients can be combined early in the day, refrigerated, and popped in the oven about an hour before dinner."

Jane and Bill Williams' comment: "This was a favorite supper dish, served to our family when we arrived for a weekend visit."

1 3½-ounce package or jar sliced smoked beef, soaked in warm water
    for 15 seconds, then drained on a paper towel and snipped with
    scissors into pieces about 1-1½ inches. Armour dried beef is
    available for this dish.

1 15-ounce can macaroni and cheese or 2 cups of your own recipe

1 3-ounce can chopped mushrooms, drained

2 ounces (1 cup) sharp cheddar cheese, coarsely grated, not packed

¼ cup chopped green pepper

1 hard-cooked egg, chopped

1 Tablespoon instant minced onion

½ teaspoon Worchestershire sauce

½ cup soft bread crumbs

2 Tablespoons butter or margarine, melted

Combine all ingredients except crumbs and butter; turn into 1-quart casserole. Combine crumbs and butter; sprinkle over top. Bake uncovered at 350 degrees for 35-40 minutes. Garnish with green pepper rings or hard-cooked egg slices. Makes 4 servings.

*Jane and Bill Williams*

# Ocea McCaw's
## Ham Loaf   1930s

    1 pound ground ham

    1½ pounds ground pork steak

    2 beaten eggs

    1 cup cracker crumbs

    1 cup milk

Mix ingredients and make into loaf. Place in baking pan. Spread prepared mustard over loaf.

Mix together:

    1 cup brown sugar

    ¼ cup water

    ¼ cup vinegar

Pour over loaf. Bake at 350 degrees for one hour. Baste occasionally with liquid from the pan.

*Sarita and Bill McCaw*

103

# Ocea McCaw's
# Turkey Ring   1940s

Dwight and Ocea McCaw raised many thousand turkeys during World War II for Thanksgiving dinners for our troops around the world. Ocea was an excellent, enthusiastic cook, always serving something new to her family and to relatives who visited. With turkeys so plentiful she enjoyed being creative.

    3 cups turkey meat, cut up

    2 cups bread crumbs

    1 cup cooked rice

    1 teaspoon salt

    ½ teaspoon paprika

    ¼ cup chopped pimiento

    4 well-beaten eggs

    ¼ cup turkey fat or butter

    3 cups turkey broth or ½ broth and ½ milk

Mix all ingredients and place in a buttered mold or a 9 x 13 pan. Refrigerate until needed: overnight is okay. Bring to room temperature and bake at 325 degrees for 30-45 minutes, until bubbly. Serve with a heated mushroom sauce from 1 can of mushroom soup and 1 Tablespoon lemon juice.

*Sarita and Bill McCaw*

# Pork Chops with Quince Jelly
## & Sauerkraut   1960s

Shake the pork chops in a bag with some flour. Melt several Tablespoons Crisco shortening in frying pan and add pork chops, cooking until nicely browned on both sides. Drain off excess fat. Add 1 jar or can saurkraut with juice, then place pork chops on top. Drop about 8 soupspoons of quince jelly over the saurkraut, place lid on skillet, and simmer about 20 minutes. These pork chops have a most intriquing flavor!

*Naomi*

# Old-Fashioned Chicken
## with Homemade Noodles   1960s

This is a hearty, satisfying winter feast. A green salad and baked apples make a rewarding dinner.

Place stewing hen in large kettle. Add water to cover by several inches. Add 1 large stalk celery sliced into ½-inch pieces and the tops from 5-6 stalks. Add 1 large onion, chopped in 1-inch pieces. Add 2-3 chicken bouillon cubes or 1-2 Tablespoons granulated chicken bouillon. Add 2 Tablespoons soy sauce. Simmer until tender.

While chicken is cooking make the noodles:
   4 large eggs
   ½ cup regular milk
   4 cups flour
   1 teaspoon salt, optional

Beat eggs and milk together and add salt and flour, mixing very well. Dough will be stiff when all the flour is added. Keep mixing until blended. Turn onto floured bread board and roll out to a rectangle ⅛ inch thick. Let rest 20 minutes. Sprinkle generously with flour, then roll as you would for a jelly roll. Slice roll in about ⅜-inch pieces, shaking each one out on the floured bread board. Let stand to dry 1-2 hours.

When chicken is done remove from broth and place on platter to cool. Remove meat from bones in large pieces. Set aside. Test broth for flavor and add more soy sauce or bouillon to your taste. Bring broth to boiling. Shake flour from noodles and add to broth. Stir gently to separate noodles. Cover and cook on medium heat about 20 minutes until done. Watch carefully to avoid boiling over, placing lid ajar to prevent this, if necessary. When noodles are done, add chicken and simmer a few minutes longer. Serves four hungry people. The real secret to this delectable dish is the soy sauce. It enhances and enriches the broth. Try this for your next Sunday dinner.

*Naomi*

# Vignettes

In her later years, Grandmother Ida seldom ventured from the house, though when early spring came, some afternoons she would invite me to come along for her special walk. We would go on our search for her favorite Jim Hill mustard greens. They grew along the roadside and the lane to the Touchet River and other special places. This was a happy expedition, and when we returned with a full basket of the wonderful greens we would prepare them for dinner that evening. Boiled only a few minutes, they made a very welcome treat enjoyed for a short time each spring.

On a very hot summer afternoon many years ago one of the horses at our cousins' ranch decided to cool off a bit. She carefully stepped into the large concrete water trough, had a long refreshing drink, and enjoyed the cool water on her legs. Half an hour later she was still there, enjoying her new-found comfort. Later it was discovered that all the goldfish were gone from the watering trough! It still remains a mystery.

At milking time, when we were small children living on Grandfather Edwin's ranch, he would take us with him in the afternoon. To our delight he would call his two large friendly cats to join us. While he was milking, the cats would stand on their hind legs beside him. He'd send a stream of milk right into their mouths. The cats, of course, loved every minute and would run to him at every milking. What fun for the cats! And fun for us to watch.

Another walk for Grandmother Ida was out to the orchard near our house in the fall to gather hazelnuts. She always knew when they were ready to be picked. Some would be on the ground and easy to gather. They were fun to find and to enjoy with our family in the evenings.

In the late fall and all winter we would have popcorn in the evening with lots of our own homemade sweet butter. It was a family tradition that we have icy cold red or yellow delicious apples to eat with the popcorn. They came from Grandfather Edwin's orchard.

# Roast Duckling
## with Chutney & Peaches   1980s

Duckling seems to be a challenge for many cooks to prepare. You will find my new method of roasting quick and easy. The duckling is free of skin and fat, succulent, and delicious.

Thaw duckling and remove giblets. Place duckling in a large pan with lukewarm water for 10 minutes to bring to room temperature. Set oven at 425 degrees. When ready to roast, line broiler pan with a piece of heavy foil, then take another piece of heavy foil 3 feet long, center it lengthwise in broiler pan with the dull side down. Remove duckling from water and pat dry inside and out. Place duckling lengthwise in the center with the breast side up. Fold foil to center and seal edges by folding over 3 or 4 times. Seal other edges of foil the same way. Place on center rack and bake in 425 degree oven for 20 minutes then at 400 degrees for 2 hours. Remove from oven and carefully open one corner of foil and drain all oil into a pan to discard.

To Carve: Cut lengthwise down center of duckling breast. Remove layer of skin and fat by sliding a carving knife under it. Remove each side breast in one piece to a warmed platter and cover. Repeat procedure with legs and thighs, also keeping in one piece. One duckling serves two or three persons.

To Serve: Place drained cling peach halves in a shallow baking dish and fill each half with a Tablespoon of Sharwood's Mango and Ginger Chutney (Indian style chutney is best). Place in microwave or conventional oven set at 400 degrees until peaches and chutney are hot. Surround duckling with peaches on serving platter or serve from baking dish.

*Naomi*

# Steve Martin's
## Oregon Coast Mussels   1990s

While vacationing on the Oregon Coast, my son Steve Martin and his family enjoyed a seafood restaurant tucked in a cove above the ocean. After enjoying the delicious mussels served there, Steve developed this recipe—Washington's answer to the New England clam bake.

Simmer for 4-6 hours:

    1 large can or 3 small cans stewed tomatoes, seasoned

    1 large green pepper cut in ¾-inch chunks

    1 large onion, cut in ¾-inch pieces

    2-3 large stalks celery, cut in 1-inch pieces

    1 small head garlic, cloves peeled

    3 bay leaves

    3 cans vegetable broth

    2-3 cups red wine

    2-4 Tablespoons butter

    5-6 pounds fresh small mussels

    Water as needed

This broth can be made ahead and refrigerated. While broth is heating, scrub mussels. When broth is boiling, add mussels and cook until all shells are opened, usually about 10 minutes. Serve mussels and broth very hot with garlic bread and green salad.

*Naomi*

*1962. When Marilyn McCaw arrived home from college for the summer, she drew this sketch. Her brother Paul thought this old wagon had character and pulled it with a team to the top of the hill behind their house. There it was silhouetted on the skyline until, about two years later, after their cattle had enjoyed frequent back rubs, the old wagon became a thing of the past.*

# Mixed Mustard   1890s

This sauce is unique and tasty. It is rather hot, but delicious with meat.

Two Tablespoonsful dry mustard, 1/4 teaspoonful salt, one teaspoonful brown sugar. Mix to a thick paste with cooking oil, about 1 Tablespoonful, and cider vinegar. Let stand 24 hours before using.

*Ladies of the Presbyterian Church Cookbook, Prescott, 1903*

# Ham Gravy   1920s

November was hog butchering time on the ranches in our valley with 30-40 hogs processed in one day, providing ham, bacon, and lots of sausage and pork chops for each family. It was a major event requiring the help of all the men, including the hired men. Freezing weather was required to keep the meat fresh until it could be cut up and processed. The ham and bacon were cured with salt, then hung in the smokehouse above a fire of applewood. I still remember the delicious warm fragrance of the smokehouse when we would open the door and bring in a ham or side of bacon for our own use. The fat from the hogs was placed in a huge iron pot hung on a tripod of poles over a bonfire, then heated until the fat was cooked and melted and the pieces of skin formed cracklings that were delicious. The fat was poured into 5-pound tin cans and stored for use in cooking.

When Marie, Ruth, and Bessie were attending Oregon State College, Grandfather Edwin would send boxes of pork chops to them by mail. I wonder what her thoughts were when the cook at their sorority house received them and knew she must prepare them for dinner. Food tasted so good when we were children and growing up! This simple recipe was a happy treat. It takes just a few minutes when you're cooking breakfast or dinner.

After frying slices of ham in a heavy iron skillet pour off the grease but try to retain all of the flavorful little bits and pieces. Add about 1 cup of whole milk and slowly bring to a simmer. Scrape up the bits from the skillet to flavor the milk. While very hot, pour over white bread.

# Sugar Cure for Meat   1930s

Nearly all of the meat on the ranches and farms was cured at home. The fragrance from the apple-wood fires and the curing meat was wonderful. After hours of baking in the old wood stoves, those hams really did taste more delicious than ours do today!

1 cup salt
1 Tablespoon red pepper
1 Tablespoon black pepper
1 Tablespoon brown sugar

Mix this amount for each piece of meat, wrap each piece in 3 yards brown paper, and place in a 100-pound flour sack. Hang with the hock down in your smokehouse, build small fire under and keep fire going until meat is well smoked and cured.

*Prescott Home Economics Club Cookbook, 1942*

# Roast Beef Sauce   1930s

1 scant teaspoon salt
1 teaspoon dry mustard
3 heaping teaspoons powdered sugar

Mix with 1 teaspoon water. Then add 2 teaspoons vinegar and 4 teaspoons Worchestershire sauce. This is delicious on hot or cold roast beef.

*Prescott Home Economics Club Cookbook, 1942*

# Autumn

Autumn in the Touchet Valley can be the best time of all. With harvest over there is an air of contentment and time to reflect, relax, and enjoy October's bright golden days. Apples and pears, black walnuts and chestnuts are ready to be picked and enjoyed.

Years ago when taking an afternoon hike, we would cross the river to find delicious white peaches in an old, old orchard, belonging to our nearest neighbor. Along the way we could hear Chinese pheasants making their "calking" sounds nearby. As we walked through the weeds, our feet released the pungent fragrance of the wild sage.

There was a large, old, wild choke cherry tree near the river and if we were on horseback, we could reach the cherries but, oh, how they made our mouths pucker! The Indians liked to find them to make pemmican for the winter.

Bob White quail, white-tailed deer, rabbits, raccoons, barn owls, and howling coyotes still make their homes in the valley. The coyotes live in caves dug into the sides of the gullies between the rounded hills and make forays to the ranches and farms in search of a tasty dinner. In the winter of 1992 cougars were seen once again after being gone for decades.

Teasel grows abundantly near the Touchet River. The Indians used it to brush their hair, and early settlers found it useful for carding wool. They would attach a number of teasel heads to a thin board with a handle, and using two of these could card the wool before spinning it into yarn. Giant old honey locust trees, with their long brown pods, and Osage Orange trees are still standing. The trees formed windbreaks that protected the large orchard planted by Grandfather Edwin McCaw.

# Cakes

# Cakes & More Cakes

Cakes and other desserts were the most enjoyable part of dinners and suppers, both for the women who baked them and for those who anticipated their arrival at the table. Angel food was often the special birthday cake for the girls in our families, while rich chocolate cakes were everyone's favorite at church suppers, family picnics, and potluck dinners.

These old cake recipes are truly delicious. They have a flavor that is unique, rich, and satisfying and taste completely different from today's cakes. Note, for example that the white cakes form a delicate topping as they bake.

Many of the recipes featured on the following pages appeared in the 1903 *Ladies of the Presbyterian Church Cookbook* and call for Snowdrift flour. That brand of flour was made at the mill in Prescott until it was destroyed by fire sometime after the turn of the century. Because every recipe in the church cookbook used Snowdrift flour, it is likely that the mill was the sponsor.

# Great Aunt Mary McCaw Erwin
## *&* Grandmother Ida McCaw's
## Cream Cake with Lemon Jelly   1867

This was Great Aunt Mary's cake recipe from about 1867, treasured and passed on from her sister Louisa Outman to her sister-in-law Ida.

Once, when Aunt Ruth McCaw Merrill was a young woman, she baked this special cake for Dr. Campbell, a family friend and the guest of honor at a church supper. With great pride she showed her cake to Dr. Campbell and placed it on the table with the others. However, before dessert was served, a woman whisked it away and served the entire cake to her sons. Aunt Ruth remembered and enjoyed this story when she was almost ninety years old, but when it happened it was no laughing matter!

This cake tastes like the very best of the old-fashioned ones made from "scratch", as our mothers used to say. It has a unique and satisfying flavor and a delicate, delicious crust on top. After all these years, this cake and filling are still favorites for our family and all of our friends.

Original Recipe (note that coffee cups are used as measures):

> Break two eggs in a coffee cup, fill the cup with sweet cream, one cup sugar, one and a half cups Snowdrift flour, one and a half teaspoonsful baking powder, flavor with vanilla, bake in layers.

Updated Version:

> Break two large eggs in a one-pint glass measuring cup, then fill the cup with sweet whipping cream until it equals 1¼ cups. Add 1 teaspoon Schilling Pure Vanilla Extract. Pour into mixing bowl and beat until well blended. Add one cup sugar and blend until smooth. Add one and one half cups Softasilk Flour that has been sifted before measuring, mixed with one and one half teaspoons baking powder, and sifted again. Then bake in layers in greased and floured cake pans at 350 degrees for 20 minutes. Let cool in pans 10 minutes, then cool on racks.

*Ladies of the Presbyterian Church Cookbook, Prescott, 1903*

# Grandmother Ida McCaw's
# Lemon Jelly for Filling & Topping  1890s

You may want to try the original recipe and double or triple it. I like to have some extra filling to spoon over the cake when serving and find the recipe using 8 eggs makes just the right amount.

Original Recipe:

> One cup sugar, two Tablespoonsful butter, two eggs, and the juice of two lemons. Beat all together and boil till the consistency of jelly.

1990 Version:

> 8 eggs
> 8 lemons
> 4 cups sugar
> ½ cup butter

Use large or extra large eggs, removing the yolk anchors from the egg whites as you break each one. Yolk anchors are the opaque solids in the egg white. To easily remove, break each egg into a shallow dish, then use a piece of the shell to cut the anchor from the yolk. Melt the butter over low heat in a heavy saucepan (stainless is best, not aluminum). Beat the eggs slightly, then add the sugar and strained lemon juice and mix well. Cook over medium heat, stirring constantly, until mixture is thickened and coats a spoon. Remove from heat and cool, then place in the refrigerator overnight. Whip 2 pints of heavy style whipping cream very stiff. Gently fold some of the whipped cream into the cold lemon jelly until you have your desired tartness. Remove the frozen layers of white cake from the freezer and place one layer on a large cake plate that can be kept in the freezer. Quickly spread a generous filling, add top layer and secure with 2 thin wooden skewers about 6 inches long placed vertically through both layers. Thickly cover the entire cake with filling mixture. It will slide down the sides a bit, but that's okay. Place in freezer. Put extra filling in container and freeze. When cake is frozen, place on bottom of large plastic cake cover or larger flat plate. Add top part of cover and close tightly. It keeps very well for several weeks in the freezer. Remove cake from freezer about twenty minutes before serving. Serve with a large spoonful of fresh raspberries on each slice and a spoonful of the extra filling over the berries.

*Ladies of the Presbyterian Church Cookbook, Prescott, 1903*

# Great Aunt Mary McCaw Erwin's
## Dried Apple Cake with Molasses   1860s

Great Aunt Mary and her husband Sam Erwin were the first of the family to move to the Prescott area from Crawfordsville in the Willamette Valley. They arrived in 1866 and began farming two miles east of Prescott near the Touchet River. Uncle Sammy had a very large orchard with many varieties of fruit and nut trees. In 1876 he wrote to his family, "My fruit crop was good this year in apples, peaches, apricots, plums and grapes. I dry fruit by the evaporation process. It is called the Plummer process. The demand for my fruit crop is very good. I sold over 50,000 pounds; we dried only about 2,000 pounds."

In the fall he would make great quantities of apple butter in a huge cast iron cauldron over an outdoor fire. Wooden barrels would be filled with this delicious jam and loaded into his wagon. Then he would make a long journey north to Canada with his team and wagon, selling the apple butter to ranchers, farmers, and Indians along the way. He would be invited to spend the night with the family whose home he reached late in the afternoon. Great Aunt Mary had lots of apples to cook with and this cake is best of all!

One cupful butter, two cups sugar, one cup milk, two eggs, one teaspoonful baking soda, three and one-half cups Snowdrift flour, two cups raisins, three cups dried apples, soaked overnight and chopped fine, then stewed two hours in two cups molasses. Beat butter and sugar to a cream, add milk in which soda has been dissolved, then the beaten eggs and flour, and lastly the apples well stirred in. Pour into pan and bake one and one-half hours at 325-350 degrees. Very good.

Note: This makes enough batter for one 9 x 13 inch glass baking dish and one 8 x 8 inch pan. Try this marvelous cake warm from the oven with vanilla ice cream.

*Ladies of the Presbyterian Church Cookbook, Prescott 1903*

# Great Aunt Mary McCaw Erwin's
## White Cake   1870s

When gold was discovered in Idaho in 1860, thousands of men needed food and supplies. Great Uncle Sam Erwin was destined to be one of the suppliers. As soon as his trees began to bear, he freighted the fruit and nuts to the mines in Kellogg, Idaho, where such luxuries were worth their weight in gold.

Adapted from the book *Wait's Mill* by Ellis and Elvira Laidlaw.
Article by Vance Orchard, *The Waitsburg Times*, Waitsburg, Washington

Three cups white sugar, half cup butter, whites of eight eggs, two cups Snowdrift flour, not measured until sifted, one teaspoonful baking powder, one cup sweet milk. Beat butter and sugar to a cream, add the flour, baking powder and milk and beat till smooth. Flavor with 20 drops almond extract or one teaspoon vanilla. Lastly fold in the well-beaten whites of the eggs and bake in layers in greased and floured pans at 350 degrees 20 minutes or until done.

Note: Freezing the layers for an hour or two before frosting keeps the cake crumbs from mixing with the frosting. Try this the next time you bake.

*Ladies of the Presbyterian Church Cookbook, Prescott, 1903*

121

# Grandmother Emma McCaw's
## Dried Apple Cake   1880s

Dried apples were available in abundance, prepared by the women in the summer and fall. Apples were often dried by laying slices on a window screen outdoors in the sun, then covering them with cheesecloth. When dried, they were carefully stored in the pantry and used for cooking in the winter and spring after the fresh apples were gone.

> Three cups dried apples, three cups white sugar, one-third cup butter, two well-beaten eggs, half cup rich buttermilk or cream, two teaspoonsful soda sifted in five cups Snowdrift flour, one teaspoonful each of cinnamon, nutmeg, and allspice.

Stew apples in water over medium-low heat. Drain apples and cool to lukewarm. Cream butter, add eggs and buttermilk or cream, and apples. Last add flour mixed with soda and spices and blend. Pour into large baking pan and bake at 350 degrees about 1 hour or until done.

*Ladies of the Presbyterian Church Cookbook, Prescott 1903*

*Years ago Bruce McCaw found this top gear and crank with press lever by the side of the road and bought them from the farmer for five dollars. He then built his cider press using the old gears that were patented in 1855 by P. P. Mast, Cleveland, Ohio.*

# Grandmother Emma McCaw's
# Chocolate Potato Cake   1890s
### *As made by Ethel Sarah McCaw Vernon in the 1930s*

Mother made Boston Baked Beans and Potato Cake for every Sunday School picnic and family reunion that I can remember. This recipe is still one of my favorites.

*For interest only –*
One half cup butter creamed with one half cup sugar. Add beaten yolks of four eggs, half cup milk, two cups sifted Snowdrift flour, one cup fresh mashed potatoes, one cup walnuts, one teaspoon each of cinnamon, cloves, and nutmeg, and two bars chocolate. Add lastly two teaspoons baking powder and the whites of four eggs.

Updated Version:
Dorothy writes: "We always stuck to the old recipe. However, it helps to use an electric mixer. Mother always used Ghirardelli ground chocolate, about a cup, or cocoa, and a bit more sugar. Pour into 3 prepared cake pans. Bake at 350 degrees for 30 minutes. Ice with caramel frosting." Indeed, this cake was always frosted with Caramel Frosting from the old Prescott recipe book contributed by Nellie Erwin.

Caramel Filling:
2 cups brown sugar, three fourths cup sweet cream, one Tablespoon vanilla, a piece of butter the size of a walnut, 2-3 Tablespoons. Cook all together till thick over medium heat. Stir to prevent scorching. Cool and beat until creamy.

Updated Creamy Caramel Icing:

      2 cups brown sugar

      1 Tablespoon butter

      1Tablespoon corn syrup

      ½ cup milk (or cream)

Boil above ingredients to 238 degrees. (Soft ball forms in cold water)

      ⅓ cup butter

      2 cups sifted confectioners sugar

      4 Tablespoons hot milk

      1 teaspoon vanilla

Combine the last four ingredients and beat until smooth. Pour hot syrup over butter mixture. Beat until thick and creamy.

*Dorothy Vernon Avril*

Alene adds: "Our mother always got requests for this cake for all the church picnics and family gatherings—McCaws and Vernons. Mother had her own special way of cutting this cake and how wonderful it was if you were the lucky child who got the center end piece with all the thick, sweet sugar icing on it."

Alene's Caramel Icing:

      2 cups brown sugar, ½ cup butter, ½ cup cream. Combine, stir, boil without

      stirring 3-5 minutes to 238 degrees—softball stage. Remove from heat.

      Beat until cool and thickened. Beat in 1 teaspoon vanilla.

# Grandmothers Louisa Outman & Ida McCaw's
# Tilden Cake   1890s

Louisa wrote this recipe in Ida's cookbook with the comment, "This recipe I have tried and know to be good. From your loving sister, Lou Outman, Spring Hollow, January the 18th, 1897."

This is a lovely, interesting cake that requires delicate measuring and mixing. Delightfully different, it is one you will bake for that special family gathering time and again. The cakes made with tender care so long ago were beautiful and always worth the extra time and effort.

Original Recipe:

> One cup butter, two cups pulverized sugar, one cup sweet milk, three cups
> Snowdrift flour, one half cup Argo corn starch, four eggs, two teaspoonsful
> baking powder, two teaspoonsful pure lemon extract.

Updated Version:

Set oven at 350 degrees. Sift the cake flour onto a large piece of waxed paper, then gently spoon the flour into the sifter. Lightly spoon into a one cup measure and level the top without packing the flour, putting this into the sifter. Repeat two more times. Sift a quantity of cornstarch onto another piece of waxed paper. Gently spoon into a ½ cup measure and level the top, again not packing down the cornstarch. Add the cornstarch to the sifted flour. Add the baking powder and mix very gently with a tablespoon then sift once more to mix. Set aside.

Beat eggs about one minute. Cream the softened butter until it is fluffy. Add sugar to butter while mixing until well blended. Add eggs and lemon flavoring. Then add ⅓ of the flour, folding in gently. Add ⅓ of the milk, again folding in gently. Repeat until all of the flour and the milk are added. Bake in 2 greased and floured round 9-inch cake pans for about 30 minutes or until done when tested with a toothpick. Cool on a rack for 10 minutes. Run a knife around edge of pan to loosen cake. Invert onto a rack, then cover with another rack and invert once more so your cake layers are right side up. This prevents cracking through the layers. Enjoy this very special cake, which really tastes like the ones grandmother used to bake.

Filling:

Take one cup of sweet cream and whip till stiff, add three Tablespoonsful sugar and 1 teaspoonful real vanilla, stir well together and spread between layers. This cake is best topped with lots of fresh sliced peaches and more whipped cream.

*Kay and Dennis Stanley*

## Nellie Erwin's
## Strawberry Shortcake    1900s

This recipe was found in the old church Cookbook and was contributed by Nellie before she was married to Bill Williams in 1908.

Sift together two cupsful Snowdrift flour, four teaspoonsful baking powder, one Tablespoonful sugar. Sift this mixture twice. Work into this one-third cup butter, and add gradually three-fourths cup milk, working together with a knife. Turn out on a board, handle as little as possible, lightly patting dough to flatten a little, then roll till about half an inch thick. Take a large biscuit cutter, cutting the dough in rounds and placing them in a pan so the dough will not run together. Bake in hot oven, 400 degrees, ten or twelve minutes. To prepare the strawberries, dip each one in water, then hull, cut in halves, sprinkle with powdered sugar, and place on back of range where berries may be warming while cakes are baking. When cakes are baked, tear them open and butter, then place a layer of berries between layers and on top and serve with whipped cream that has a little sugar and vanilla added.

*Ladies of the Presbyterian Church Cookbook, Prescott, 1903*

# Grandmother Mae McCaw's
# Orange Cake with Sauce   1910s

This was one of Grandmother's favorite recipes.

Juice of ½ lemon and 1 orange

⅓ cup shortening, butter is best

¼ teaspoon salt

1½ cups sugar

1 egg

1 cup buttermilk with 1 teaspoon soda added to milk

2 cups flour

1 cup raisins, measured and ground

Mix juices with ½ cup sugar and set aside. Grind orange and lemon peel with the raisins. Cream sugar and shortening, add the beaten egg, milk and sugar, then the flour and fruit. Bake in a shallow pan, which has been greased and floured, about 40 minutes at 350 degrees. While hot, pour all of the juice over the top of the cake in the pan. Serve from the pan.

*Jerrianne Powell*

# Nellie Erwin Williams' Fruit Cake   1910s

Nellie and her husband Bill lived just over the hills in the next valley north of the Touchet Valley. Nellie was a favorite cousin and is remembered for her warmth and kindness. The women in the McCaw families spent many happy hours together at church suppers, picnics, quilting bees, and reunion celebrations.

Original Recipe:

One pound butter, one pound brown sugar, one pound sifted Snowdrift flour, three pounds stoned raisins, three pounds currants, one pound citron, one dozen eggs, half cup molasses, two Tablespoonsful cinnamon, one Tablespoonful rose extract (available at a pharmacy), two small teaspoonsful cloves, one half of a whole nutmeg grated and the grated peel of one lemon. Beat yolks together, add beaten whites alternately with flour, spice, fruit and citron. Also add a wine glass full of coffee. Roll fruit in flour before adding.

Jane Lust Williams has converted the above quantities to standard measure:

2 cups butter

2⅔ cups brown sugar

4 cups flour

8 cups seedless raisins

8 cups currants

1 pound citron

1 dozen eggs

½ cup molasses

2 Tablespoons cinnamon

1 Tablespoon rose extract

2 scant teaspoons cloves

1½ teaspoons nutmeg

grated peel of 1 lemon

½ cup coffee

*Jane and Bill Williams*

# September Hayride

*Waitsburg, Washington Territory*

September 10, 1889
Editor, *Waitsburg Times*

The social event of the season occurred this evening. A goodly number of Waitsburg's young people representing "her beauty and her chivalry" assembled in the spacious domain of a hayrack and drawn by a "four in hand" set out on an expedition to the ranch of Mr. Samuel Erwin, some seven miles from town. The company set out in very hilarious spirits, and the flow of humor did not abate for a moment during the whole time. A short distance from town two gentlemen (?) on horseback kindly undertook to lead the way, and observing that the dust was deep and the expedition heavily laden, they endeavored to make it lighter for the horses by kicking all the dust on the road into the air. How thoughtful some men are! On the way out the company enjoyed themselves in songs "Comesy Come", "Repeated Alliteration," etc., and while at Mr. Erwin's the time was wholly employed in getting on the outside of peaches, grapes and watermelon. One of the especial duties of the reporter was to count the number of peaches a certain professional man in the party "got away with." Unfortunately after having filled several blank books with dots, each dot representing a devoured peach, he lost the count, and the extent of the Dr.'s feat will never be known. On the homeward journey the company developed wonderful ability to say witty things. Indeed, so witty did the party become that the hat of one young man became so hilarious it emigrated from its owner's head to the road, and literally rolled in the dust for very laughter. To be sure, the end of the whip stock in the hand of a young lady was seen to pass in close proximity to the head of the young man at the time the hat left its owner's cranium, but of course that was not the cause of its sudden flight. Another characteristic of the company was to look on the bright side of things. Once when the cloud of dust was so dense that it shut out the stars and made the moon look like a green cheese in the bottom of the Missouri river, someone remarked, "There is one good thing about this country; there are no stumps in the road." This remark had scarcely been made when a portion of stumps was run over with jolts and jarrings; but still a bright side could be found. "There may be some stumps, one thing is sure, there are no mud puddles."

The party at last arrived home at a reasonable hour. On account of the amiable qualities of the company and the kindness of Mr. Erwin, a most enjoyable time was spent in spite of the dust and bad roads, and if anyone was asked if he were sorry he went, the answer would invariably be "No"! The party consisted of the following: Reverend Jamieson and wife, W. B. Schaffer and wife, A. L. Storie and wife, Mrs. Carrie Payne, Mrs. Fannie Dumass, and Misses Lizzie Ibberson, Mabel Boorman, Marietta Wickersham, Alta Wickersham, Mary Jessup and Anna Jessup; Messrs. Hazelhurst, Russell, Laidlaw, Schaffer, McKinney, Dickinson, Storie and Loundagin.

# Nellie Erwin Williams'
# Yellow Angel Food Cake   1910s

This is an excellent companion recipe to Nellie's White Angel Food Cake, using the whole dozen eggs. Bill remembers: "Young farm wives faced certain difficulties keeping their kitchens running smoothly. Mother was often fussing with the big old wood range to keep the fire going. 'Oh, Shoot!' was heard quite often, when she was baking cakes, pies, and cookies."

1 cup egg yolks

1 Tablespoon lemon juice and 1 teaspoon vanilla with enough water to equal
      ½ cup

Blend together egg yolks and water mixture.

Add 1 cup sugar.

Beat on high speed for 15 minutes.

Gradually add 1½ cups flour to egg mixture and blend.

Mix ¼ teaspoon salt and some of grated lemon rind with flour.

Fold flour gently into egg mixture with wire whip as for White Angel Food cake. Bake 50 minutes at 325 degrees and ten minutes at 350 degrees.

Let cool in pan, then remove to rack to cool.

*Jane and Bill Williams*

# Nellie Erwin William's
# White Angel Food Cake   1910s

This delicious cake was traditionally baked for all our family birthdays.

    1 cup sugar
    1 cup egg whites
    ⅔ cup cake flour
    1 scant teaspoon cream of tartar
    Pinch of salt
    1 teaspoon vanilla

Sift flour 3 times and set aside. Beat egg whites, cream of tartar, salt and vanilla with wire whip until foamy. Gradually add sugar and continue beating until meringue holds stiff peaks. Fold flour in gently just until the flour disappears. Pour into angel food cake pan and bake 35 to 45 minutes in 350 degree oven. Let stand upside down until cold, then remove from pan.

*Jane and Bill Williams*


# Nellie Erwin Williams'
# Walnut Filling   1910s

Half cup chopped walnut meats, half cup thick sour cream, half cup sugar.
Beat well and flavor with vanilla.

Jane Williams' Note:
I used commercial sour cream and found the consistency was not spreadable but was very tasty. I think regular old sour cream would work! Add a little regular cream or whole milk to spread. 1 teaspoon or less vanilla is good.

*Jane and Bill Williams*

## Nellie Erwin Williams' Caramel Filling   1910s

Two cups brown sugar, three-fourths cup sweet cream, one Tablespoonful vanilla, a piece of butter the size of a walnut. Cook all together till thick. Stir to prevent scorching.

Jane Williams' Note:
Would recommend cooking in double boiler. After cooking, beat vigorously and cool. One Tablespoon butter could equal a walnut.

## Nellie Erwin Williams' Milk & Sugar Icing   1910s

To one cup sugar add four Tablespoonsful sweet milk and let boil four minutes. Remove from stove and add one teaspoonful vanilla and beat until creamy.

Jane Williams' Note:
Try not to overbeat icing. White vanilla would make a white icing; regular vanilla made a light beige one. Recipe is enough for only 1 dozen cupcakes. Very sweet.

## Nellie Erwin Williams' Filling for Devil's Cake   1910s

One cup brown sugar, one cup water, one Tablespoonful vinegar. Boil until thick like candy and stir into this the beaten whites of two eggs and a quarter pound marshmallows, boil up again and put on cake.

Jane Williams' Note:
One-quarter pound marshmallows equals 16 large ones or 2 cups miniature ones. Boiling time is 20 to 25 minutes. This frosting makes the right amount for a 3-layer cake. Cut recipe in half for 2 layers.

*Jane and Bill Williams*

# Grandmother Amanda McCaw Erwin
## & Nellie Erwin Williams' War Cake   1914-18

Jane Williams writes: "This recipe originated some time during World War I and was called "milkless, butterless, eggless cake." Our family likes this version because there is as much cake as fruit."

2 cups brown sugar

3 Tablespoons lard

1 teaspoon cinnamon

2 cups boiling water

1 pound raisins (2 cups)

½ teaspoon cloves

Mix and boil 5 minutes. Let stand until thoroughly cold. Add 3 cups flour and 1 teaspoon soda dissolved in a little hot water. Add 1 cup broken walnuts and other fruit as desired. Pour into greased and floured loaf pans and bake 1 hour in 325 degree oven.

Caramel frosting is wonderful on this unusual cake.

*Jane and Bill Williams and Della Mae Erwin Sanders*

# Virgil Shupe's
# Gingerbread   1920s

Connie Shupe Plants tried this recipe from her father and said that it turned out great and her family really enjoyed it—just like old times!

½ cup butter or margarine

½ cup brown sugar

½ cup Brer Rabbit Gold Brand Molasses

½ cup boiling water

1½ cups flour, unsifted

1 teaspoon baking soda

¼ teaspoon salt

½ teaspoon ground ginger

¼ teaspoon ground mace

½ teaspoon cinnamon

1 egg, beaten

Put molasses into mixing bowl with butter and sugar. Pour in boiling water, stir well and let cool. Add spices, baking soda, and salt to flour and sift together. Add beaten egg and mix well. Turn into a well-greased and floured 9" x 9" Pyrex pan and bake at 350 degrees for 30 minutes. A metal baking pan or muffin tins would require less baking time. Serve warm with whipped cream with vanilla and sugar added.

*Connie and Clyde Plants*

# Lovers' Wedding Cake

Four pounds of flour of love, one and one half pounds of buttered youth, one and one half pounds of sweet temper, one and one half pounds of self forgetfulness, one and one half pounds of powdered wits, one and one half ounces of dry humor, two tablespoonfuls of sweet argument, one and one half pints of rippling laughter, one and one half wineglassfuls of common sense. Put the flour of love, good looks and sweet temper into a well furnished house. Beat the butter of youth to cream. Mix together blindness of faults, self forgetfulness, powdered wits, dry humor into sweet argument, then add them to the above. Pour in gently rippling laughter and common sense. Work it together until all is well mixed, then bake gently forever.

*M. R. B.*

This delightful recipe was found between the pages of Grandmother Ida McCaw's diary from the early 1930s.

# Ethel Michelsen McCaw's
# Mashed Potato Cake   1920s

Ethel enjoyed baking this moist chocolate cake with the recipe from Emma McCaw. Potatoes were often included in cakes for their added moisture, texture, and flavor.

¾ cup Crisco shortening

1¾ cup sugar

¾ cup lukewarm mashed potatoes

3 cups flour sifted 4 times

4 teaspoons baking powder

½ teaspoon salt

3 eggs

¾ cup milk

2½ squares baking chocolate, melted

½ cup broken nut meats

1 teaspoon vanilla

Cream shortening and sugar. Add mashed potatoes, milk, and eggs. Next add flour with baking powder and salt added. Last add chocolate, vanilla, and nuts. Bake at 350 degrees.

Note: When you are preparing the cake pans for baking a chocolate cake, sift some unsweetened cocoa powder over the shortening rather than flour. It will keep the cake chocolate colored.

*Lois McCaw Ellsaesser*

# Jean Erwin's
# Angel Cake   1920s

One glass Snowdrift flour, one and one half glasses sugar, one Tablespoonful orange juice, one teaspoonful cream of tartar, whites of one dozen eggs. Sift flour once before measuring, fill the glass and shake down twice and fill up, add cream of tartar and sift five times, sift sugar the same. If eggs are small use thirteen. Beat eggs to a stiff froth, add sugar slowly and then flour in same manner. Add the orange juice. Bake in a new eight-quart angel food pan without any grease, covered with another pan until almost done. Bake 35 or 40 minutes in a moderate oven, 325-350 degrees.

A favorite glass was often used in measuring. Usually it equaled about 1-1½ standard measuring cups.

*Ladies of the Presbyterian Church Cookbook, Prescott, 1903*

# Katherine Holling McCaw's
# Angel Food Cake   1920s

The original recipe came from Grandmother Amanda Erwin and her daughter Margaret. Numerous tasty renditions have been enjoyed through the years at various celebrations, particularly birthdays.

Separate 12 or 13 eggs to get enough egg whites to fill one large green glass. Put egg whites in a large oval platter and whip with a whisk until foamy. Sprinkle one teaspoon cream of tartar over whites then whisk until stiff. Fold in one green glass full of sugar, a pinch of salt, juice of one squeezed orange, and vanilla for flavoring. Lastly, fold in a scant green glass full of cake flour. Spoon batter into an ungreased tube pan. Place pan into a cold oven then turn the oven on to 350 degrees and bake for one hour. Take the cake from the oven and rest it upside down until cool.

Kathleen comments:
Due to the loss of the green glass and the antique oval platter and the prevalence of electric mixers, the following modern rendition has been made so that a sweet tradition can continue.

1½ cups egg whites

1½ teaspoons cream of tartar

1½ cups sugar

⅛ teaspoon salt

Juice from one orange

1 teaspoon vanilla

1¼ cups cake flour

Whip the egg whites and cream of tartar with electric mixer. Gradually add sugar and whip until whites are stiff and glossy. Add in salt, juice, and vanilla. Fold in sifted cake flour. Pour batter into tube pan and bake as directed above.

*Kathleen McCaw Bergevin and Cristy Bergevin*

*1944. During World War II newlyweds Bill and Jane Williams celebrated his first leave with a family picnic at the park in Dayton. Bill's mother Nellie and sisters Mildred and Lula arrived carrying family favorites, including that delicious angel food cake.*

# Joy Erwin Sanders'
# Angel Food Cake   1930s

Joy used a wood and coal range for years and this was when she started the cake in a cool oven. She loved decorating cakes for all our birthdays and family celebrations.

> 1⅔ cup egg whites
> Beat egg whites

Add to the whites when they get frothy:
> 1⅔ teaspoons cream of tartar
> ½ teaspoon salt

Beat whites until they are fine grained and glossy and stand in stiff peaks but are not dry.
> 1⅞ cups sugar
> 1 teaspoon vanilla
> 1¼ cups sifted cake flour

Add 1¼ cups of the sugar and the vanilla to the beaten whites. Then gently fold in the remaining sugar and the flour which has been sifted together 3 times.

Start the cake in practically a cool oven—never over 300 degrees. At the end of 20 minutes cake should rise but not brown. Bake 1 hour to 1¼ hours at 300 degrees.

*Della Mae Sanders*

# Ethel Michelsen McCaw's
# Prize White Cake   1930s

Of the cakes that Mother made, this was one of our favorites. A real prize winner! Good with fudge frosting.

½ cup Crisco shortening

1½ cups sugar

2½ cups cake flour

¼ teaspoon salt

1 cup cold water

1 teaspoon vanilla

3 teaspoons baking powder

3 egg whites

Cream sugar and Crisco shortening. Sift flour before measuring and retain ½ cup. Add flour and water, then ½ cup reserved flour mixed with baking powder and salt. Add vanilla and egg whites last, the egg whites beaten until stiff. Bake at 375 degrees for 25 minutes.

*Lois McCaw Ellsaesser*

# Icing for Decorating Cakes

This simple icing recipe can be used with virtually any kind of cake. Try it with some of your favorites.

> 1 cup Crisco shortening
>
> 8 cups powdered sugar
>
> ¾ cup skim milk
>
> 2 teaspoons vanilla
>
> ½ teaspoon salt

Frost thinly once and then frost 2nd time.

*Jerrianne Powell*


# Ocea McCaw's
# Boil & Bake Cake   1930s

Boil together 5 minutes:

> 2 cups brown sugar
>
> 2 cups water
>
> ⅔ cup shortening
>
> 2 cups raisins
>
> 2 teaspoons cinnamon
>
> 1 teaspoon cloves

When cool add:

> 1 teaspoon soda
>
> 1 teaspoon baking powder
>
> 3 cups flour
>
> 1 cup nut meats

Bake at 350 degrees 35-40 minutes in a 9 x 13 pan, greased and floured.

# Ocea McCaw's
## Caramel Fudge Frosting   1930s

Boil to soft-ball stage—238 degrees

> 1⅓ cups brown sugar
>
> 2 teaspoons shortening (butter)
>
> 2 teaspoons light corn syrup
>
> ⅓ cup milk

Combine:

> ¼ cup shortening (butter)
>
> 2 Tablespoons hot milk
>
> 1⅔ cups powdered sugar

Beat together and mix into hot syrup till creamy.  Frost cake while mix is still warm.

*Sarita and Bill McCaw*


# Ruth McCaw Merrill's
## Caramel Filling for Layer Cake   1930s

This creamy, rich filling is delightful with chocolate, white, or spice cake. Have fun trying various combinations.

> 3 cups brown sugar
>
> 1 cup cream
>
> ½ cup butter

Boil together until a thick cream, 238-240 degrees, stirring all the time and then one stir while another spreads on cake.

*Ida McCaw's Collection 1896—Dennis and Kay Stanley*

# Thanksgiving on the Farm

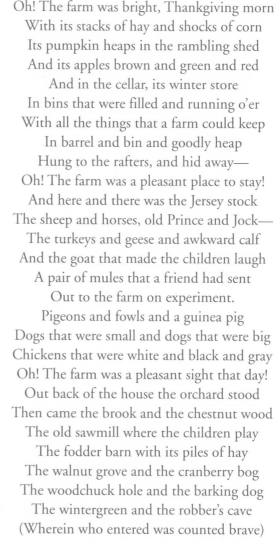

Oh! The farm was bright, Thankgiving morn
With its stacks of hay and shocks of corn
Its pumpkin heaps in the rambling shed
And its apples brown and green and red
And in the cellar, its winter store
In bins that were filled and running o'er
With all the things that a farm could keep
In barrel and bin and goodly heap
Hung to the rafters, and hid away—
Oh! The farm was a pleasant place to stay!
And here and there was the Jersey stock
The sheep and horses, old Prince and Jock—
The turkeys and geese and awkward calf
And the goat that made the children laugh
A pair of mules that a friend had sent
Out to the farm on experiment.
Pigeons and fowls and a guinea pig
Dogs that were small and dogs that were big
Chickens that were white and black and gray
Oh! The farm was a pleasant sight that day!
Out back of the house the orchard stood
Then came the brook and the chestnut wood
The old sawmill where the children play
The fodder barn with its piles of hay
The walnut grove and the cranberry bog
The woodchuck hole and the barking dog
The wintergreen and the robber's cave
(Wherein who entered was counted brave)

The skating pond with its fringe of bay
Oh! The farm was a pleasant place to stay!
The big home barn was a place of joy
For the romping girl and the climbing boy
With beams and mows and ladders to mount
Horses and oxen and sheep to count
Hunting of nests of sly old hens
Tunnelling hay and fashioning dens
Helping the men to do up the chores
Shutting windows and locking the doors
Letting some work come in with the play
Oh! The farm was a jolly place to stay!
Oh! The pantry shelves were loaded down
With cakes that were plump and rich and brown
With apple pies and pumpkin and mince
And jellies and jams and preserved quince
Cranberry sauce and puddings and rice
The dessert dishes that look so nice
Vegetables, breads, and bonbons sweet
A great brown turkey and plates of meat
Sauces fixed in the daintiest way—
Oh! 'Twas a glorious sight that day!
Oh! The farm was bright, Thanksgiving morn
The sun shone clear on the hay and corn
The guests came early with laugh and shout
And the boys and girls scattered about
Seeking the pets they had known before
Climbing through window instead of door
Racing from barn to corn crib or mill
Shouting and laughing with glee, until
The dinner bell sounded. Oh! I say,
'Twas pleasant upon the farm that day!

# Pies, Puddings & Desserts

## Pies

## Puddings

# Fruit Desserts

# Ice Cream

# Great Grandmother Sarah's
# Celebration Pie   1850s

In 1853, when Sarah and William McCaw were living in the Willamette Valley, they hosted a wedding dinner for Jane Grey and Robert Glass, a nearby neighbor. Few luxuries existed, and when it came time to prepare the dinner there was nothing from which to make a pie—no squash, pumpkin, or fruit. Instead, Sarah made several pies from beans that were first boiled and then mashed, mixed with milk, eggs, sugar, and spices and baked like pumpkin pies. All the guests declared bean pie to be a great success.
(From *250 Years of McCaws* by Robert H. McCaw)

For each pie:

      2 cups well-done white beans

      1 cup brown sugar

      ½ teaspoon salt

      2 rounded teaspoons cinnamon

      1 rounded teaspoon nutmeg

      1 rounded teaspoon cloves

      3 eggs, slightly beaten

      1½ cups rich milk, heated

Cook, drain, and vigorously mash beans until smooth and creamy. Cool to lukewarm. Beat eggs, add sugar and spices. Add mashed beans with heated milk and mix well. Pour into unbaked pie shell and bake at 425 degrees for 15 minutes, then 350 degrees for about 35 minutes until a table knife inserted in the center comes out clean. Serve chilled with whipped cream. Adding vanilla and sugar to taste makes the whipped cream more interesting.

*Ruth and Robert McCaw*

# Grandmother Ida McCaw's
# Pioneer Vinegar Pie   1890s

Marie's note: "Mother always used nutmeg and a little vanilla. It has a wonderful flavor and is perfect to pour over plain cake. Do try it—it is good and also cheap. It tastes almost like lemon pie! "

    4 large eggs, beaten
    ½ cup cider vinegar
    1½ cups sugar
    2 pinches salt
    4 Tablespoons flour
    2 cups boiling water
    ½ teaspoon nutmeg
    1 teaspoon vanilla
    ½-1 cup raisins
    1 cup whipping cream

Mix sugar, flour, and salt. Add vinegar and room temperature eggs, mixing well. Add boiling water very slowly, while stirring. Cook over medium-medium low heat. Boil gently 3-4 minutes. Remove from stove and add nutmeg, vanilla, and raisins. Cool to room temperature. Beat cream and fold gently into mixture. Pour into baked pie shell. Chill until cold. Serve with softly beaten whipped cream with sugar and vanilla added and a sprinkle of nutmeg.

Note: The wonderful flavor of this pie will surprise and delight you. The recipe is over one hundred years old. I wish I had discovered it long ago.

I have also tried the recipe with beaten egg yolks only and found the texture to be different but even more interesting. Be creative!

*Naomi*

# Marie McCaw Stanley's
# Marshmallow Chocolate Fudge Pie   1920s

This rich, creamy pie really tastes like chocolate fudge. After an afternoon of sledding and tobogganing on the big wheat hills behind Grandfather Edwin's orchard with cousins, friends, and teachers from Prescott, we would gather at our house for Mother's homemade chili and this special pie. We were terribly hungry but wouldn't end our play in the snow until we were too cold to move, not wanting to miss a minute of the best of winter fun!

½ cup flour

1 cup sugar

¼ teaspoon salt

1½ cups milk

½ cup whipping cream

1 large egg, slightly beaten

3 Tablespoons butter

12 marshmallows cut in quarters

4 squares Bakers unsweetened baking chocolate, melted

1 Tablespoon Schilling Pure Vanilla Extract

Mix flour, sugar, and salt. Add milk, cream and egg and blend. Add butter and cook in double boiler until thick, stirring all the while. This makes it creamy and smooth. Remove from heat, add marshmallows and warm chocolate, and stir until marshmallows are completely melted. Add vanilla and pour into a baked pie shell. Cool to room temperature and refrigerate. When cold, top with whipped cream that has sugar and vanilla added to your taste. This pie filling can be served in pretty dishes by itself, without the crust.

Note: For a delicious variation, whip 1 cup cream and blend into ½ of the fudge mixture. The flavor is delicate and wonderful!

*Naomi*

# Marie McCaw Stanley's
# Famous Chess Pie   1930s

Mother served this marvelous pie in individual tart shells and I believe it was her favorite dessert. She enjoyed making and sharing it with her family and friends. When talking about cooking long ago, everyone remembered this very special pie of Marie's and asked for her recipe.

2 cups sour cream

1 cup sugar

4 large eggs

3 Tablespoons flour

½ teaspoon salt

1 cup raisins

1 cup broken walnuts

butter the size of 2 walnuts—3 Tablespoons

2 teaspoons Schilling Pure Vanilla Extract

1 pint whipping cream

Make baked pie shell or small individual pie shells. Prepare filling by mixing together the slightly beaten eggs, sour cream, sugar, flour, and salt. Cook over medium heat, stirring constantly until thickened. Remove from stove. Add butter, raisins, walnuts, and vanilla. Cool, then refrigerate. When cold, whip cream and fold gradually into the filling in the amount you wish, beginning with 1 cup of whipped cream. This makes the filling light and wonderful.

*Naomi*

# Summertime
# Raspberry Pie   1980s

In 1987 we were living south of San Francisco and I arrived at the Seattle airport carrying two crates of carefully wrapped fresh raspberries to take home for a special treat. While checking in, I set the berries on the floor in front of me, just under the ticket counter. Before I could stop her, a toddler dashed under the counter, running across the berries. When I got home, I opened the package and found her footprints in the squashed berries!

    4½ cups fresh raspberries

    4 Tablespoons instant tapioca

    1⅓ cups sugar

    1 Tablespoon butter

    2 teaspoons fresh lemon juice

Wash raspberries and drain on paper towels. Mix sugar and tapioca and gently mix with berries. Pour into unbaked pie shell. Add butter cut in pieces. Sprinkle lemon juice over fruit mixture. Add top crust, then cut slits in pastry. Put strips of aluminum foil around edges to slow the browning. Remove foil when pie is nearly done.

Note: The pie crust recipe can be doubled for easier handling. Before adding the top crust, wet your fingertips with water and brush the edge of the bottom crust to seal. Then gently press the two crusts together and decorate with the tines of a dinner fork or in your favorite manner.

*Naomi*

155

# Divinity Meringue
## for Lemon Pie   1990s

Meringue has intrigued me for many years. In the spring of 1994 I found this recipe which is the one I have been searching for! Made like divinity with a sugar syrup, the meringue is creamy and delicate.

⅔ cup sugar

2 large or extra large egg whites, at room temperature

¼ teaspoon cream of tartar

1 teaspoon Schilling Pure Vanilla Extract

After the lemon filling is poured into the pie shell, cool at room temperature and place in the refrigerator while making this meringue.

In a small saucepan, combine sugar with ½ cup water. Bring to a boil, stirring occasionally. Cook over medium-high heat without stirring until syrup registers 240 degrees and is at the soft-ball stage, about 5 minutes. Remove syrup from heat and set aside.

In a large mixing bowl, beat egg whites with an electric mixer on medium speed until frothy. Add cream of tartar and beat on high speed just until soft peaks form. Return syrup to heat until it boils. Gradually pour hot syrup into egg whites (but not directly onto the beaters) while beating constantly. Continue beating while adding vanilla until egg whites are cool and very stiff, about 5 minutes.

Remove pie from refrigerator and spread meringue over the top, sealing to the edge of the crust and swirling on top. Place the pie under the broiler for 1 to 2 minutes, or until lightly browned. Let cool to room temperature, then refrigerate until the filling has set (5 to 8 hours).

This meringue recipe is used with the permission of *Eating Well, the Magazine of Food and Health*, copyright 1994.

*Naomi*

# Great Grandmother Sarah's
# Steamed Suet Pudding   1850s

This is our oldest known McCaw family recipe, which dates to the time when our great grandparents settled in Crawfordsville, Oregon Territory. Suet was used many ways in cooking because it was plentiful and cost little or nothing. Suet was probably used in the winter when it could be stored for some time and would stay fresh and mild.

One cup stoned and chopped raisins, one cup finely chopped suet, one cup brown sugar, one cup sour milk, one teaspoon soda, and 2¼ cups Snowdrift flour to stir it quite stiff like bread. Steam three hours. Berries or currants can be used instead of raisins. I steam mine in a five pound lard bucket. Very good.

Kay Stanley's Notes: Pudding is just right in a 1½ quart mold. We like this served warm with Christmas Carrot Pudding Brown Sugar Sauce.

To sour fresh milk, add 1 Tablespoon lemon juice to 1 cup milk. Lightly spoon flour into measuring cup. Spoon pudding into two 1-pound coffee cans, filling each one half full. Cover with foil or parchment and tie with string to secure. Place on low rack in large kettle with water reaching half way up sides of cans. Replace lid and steam three hours in gently boiling water.

*Ladies of the Presbyterian Church Cookbook, Prescott, 1903*

# Grandmother Amanda McCaw Erwin's
## Mincemeat   1880s

**D**ella Mae writes: "My sister, Joy Erwin, enjoyed making mincemeat with this old recipe from Grandmother."

This recipe will test your creativity! One bowl can equal 1 cup or more. For the 1-cup bowl, try 1-2 teaspoons of each spice. You can make a little or a lot of this one!

4 bowls of apples

1 bowl of cider vinegar

3 bowls of raisins

1 bowl of meat (cooked beef that has been put through food chopper)

1 bowl of sugar

1 bowl of currants

Flavor to taste with cinnamon, cloves, nutmeg, and cook until apples are well done. Neck meat is best, boiled then chopped.

*Della Mae Erwin Sanders*

*1915. After hog butchering the fat was cut from the meat and rendered into lard. A fire was built under the huge cast iron cauldron and the fat would liquify. It was then poured into pails and stored for later use. The bits of skin left over were called cracklings. When lard was being rendered doughnuts were made and fried in the hot fat. Enjoying this doughnut party are: (left to right)) Prescott teacher, Guy McCaw, Emmaline McCaw, Jay McCaw, teacher, Edith McCaw, Sam McCaw, Ethel McCaw, Robert C. McCaw, and Glen McCaw (sitting on top of the woodpile with Harry McCaw and a friend of the family).*

# Grandmother Amanda McCaw Erwin's
## Plain Custard 1880s

Plain custard requires 1 egg and 1 Tablespoon sugar to 1 cup milk and a pinch of salt (½ teaspoon of cornstarch added to the sugar helps make the custard stand firm). Place baking dish of custard in a pan of water. Bake in moderate oven but watch it closely at finish. Baking too long makes the custard watery.

Notes from Jane Lust Williams:
I scalded the milk because we always do. A pinch of salt probably equals ¼ teaspoon. I also sprinkled nutmeg on top and didn't add raisins. That would be more like rice or bread pudding. I baked the custard 1 hour at 325 degrees in a 1½ quart casserole. This recipe would serve 4 to 6 people if tripled. Very good, and cornstarch does make the consistency firm.

*Della Mae Erwin Sanders*

# Grandmother Amanda McCaw Erwin's
## Snow Pudding   1880s

Jane Lust Williams writes: "I took this pudding of Grandmother's to our church potluck and our minister proclaimed it delicious!"

One half box gelatine dissolved in one pint boiling water, add one cup sugar, juice of one lemon, strain, add whites of three eggs beaten to a stiff froth, beat all thoroughly and quickly, pour into a mold: serve cold with soft custard made of the yolks of three eggs, one small teaspoonful corn starch stirred into one pint boiling milk. Cook slowly until thick. Sweeten to taste and flavor with one teaspoon lemon extract. It is very nice.

Note from Jane:
Had to make this a second time and then checked it with an old cookbook before coming up with a workable recipe.

½ box of old fashioned gelatine equals 2 packages of Knox gelatine we use today. Before adding the stiffly beaten egg whites, allow the gelatine mixture to begin to thicken. I used ¼ cup sugar to sweeten the soft custard.

*Ladies of the Presbyterian Church Cookbook, Prescott, 1903*

# Grandmother Amanda McCaw Erwin's
## Suet Pudding  1890s

If you want to feel like a pioneer, you can make this unusual pudding. Suet is available at meat markets.

One cup chopped suet, one cup fresh prunes, two cups Snowdrift flour, one teaspoon baking powder, about one half cup sweet milk to make very stiff dough. Tie in cloth, drop in kettle of boiling water and cover with a saucer bottom side up in kettle.

Note: I tried this recipe and found it interesting. I tied the pudding in a small dishcloth. The challenge came when trying to keep the inverted plate over the pudding to keep it covered by the boiling water. The pudding was quite delicious served warm with cream.

*Ladies of the Presbyterian Church Cookbook, Prescott 1903*

# Grandmother Ida McCaw's
# Blackberry Juice Pudding   1890s

Tangled wild blackberry vines grew near the hills and across the fields in the Touchet Valley. The sun-warmed fragrance of the berries made picking them a joy, even though the thorns guarding them were very sharp!

1 cup fresh blackberry juice

1½ cups flour

1 cup sugar

¾ cup butter

4 eggs, beaten

3 Tablespoons sweet cream

1 teaspoon baking soda

Cream butter, add sugar, eggs, cream, and berry juice. Mix baking soda and flour together and add. Bake in a pan at 350 degrees about 30 minutes and eat quite warm with sauce made from the berries, vanilla ice cream, sweet cream, or the custard sauce described below.

Custard Sauce: Combine:

1 cup sugar

1 cup whipping cream

¼ cup butter

1 egg yolk

In heavy pan, melt butter, then add sugar and cream. Cook over medium heat, stirring constantly. Bring to a good rolling boil and boil 1 minute. Slowly stir hot mixture into beaten egg yolk. Return to heat, bring to boiling, and remove. Add 1 teaspoon real vanilla. Cool, then refrigerate. This delightful sauce is wonderful served over fruit cobblers, fruit puddings, and fresh fruit pies. If you wish to make this dessert when blackberries are not in season, you can use frozen or canned berries.

*Kay and Dennis Stanley*

# Grandmother Ida McCaw's
## Coconut Cream Tapioca Pudding  1890s

This pudding is another grand old-fashioned dessert. Before Grandmother Ida and Grandfather Edwin moved from Crawfordsville, Oregon, to the Touchet Valley, Ida collected favorite recipes from her relatives and friends to enjoy in her new home. Each person who sent a recipe added little notes, something Grandmother surely treasured. Her friend Addie Athow wrote: "The best wishes of one who feels thankful for this acquaintance, ever regretting its shortness, be with you always. July 9, 1896."

Soak 3 Tablespoons tapioca in water overnight. Drain and put in a quart of boiling milk and simmer ½ hour. Beat yolks of 4 eggs with one cup sugar. Add 3 Tablespoons coconut, then stir and boil 10 minutes longer. Put in a pudding dish. Beat the whites of the eggs to a stiff froth with 3 Tablespoons sugar. Pour over the top, then sprinkle with coconut over all. Set in oven to brown. Watch carefully. Serve without sauce.

Update:
Pudding can be set in 400 degree oven for 3-5 minutes and then browned under broiler. Watch carefully. Pudding is best served cold.

*Ruth McCaw Merrill*

164

# Grandmother Ida McCaw's
# Rice Cream   1890s

Comment to Ida from Elizabeth Borst, her cousin in Centralia, Washington: "These are a few recipes I copied from my mother's recipe book on leaving home and hope you will have as good luck as I have had making them. July 11, 1896."

½ cup rice

1 quart milk

3 eggs

A little salt

Sweeten to taste

A small piece of butter and flavor

Parboil the rice in a kettle of water, drain liquid, measure 1½ cups, then add most of the milk, beat up the yolks and add to them the sugar, butter, and remainder of the milk. When rice comes to a boil add yolks, etc. Then let it boil for a minute or two. Take the whites, which have been beaten stiff, and stir into the rice. In a few moments remove from the stove. Eat cold.

Kay's Note: For a smaller pudding I used:

1 cup cooked rice

3 cups milk

1 Tablespoon butter, added to rice and milk while heating

2 eggs

¼ cup sugar

¼ teaspoon salt

1 teaspoon real vanilla, added just before beaten egg whites

We liked a sprinkling of nutmeg and cinnamon. Good cold or hot for breakfast. Cold raspberry syrup drizzled over pudding is delightful!

*Kay and Dennis Stanley*

# McCaw Sisters'
## Christmas Carrot Pudding   1920s

This delicious pudding was our family's favorite for the holidays and one that the McCaw sisters—Marie, Bessie, and Ruth—served to their families for many years.

    2 cups grated carrots
    2 cups grated potatoes
    2 cups flour
    2 cups raisins
    2 cups sugar
    1 cup butter
    2 teaspoons soda
    2 teaspoons cloves
    2 teaspoons cinnamon

Cream softened butter, add sugar, and beat until fluffy. Using a grater with small holes, prepare carrots and potatoes. Lightly pack, measure, and add to butter mixture. Lightly spoon unsifted flour into measuring cup and level top. Add spices and soda to flour and gently mix, then add to carrot mixture and stir until well blended. Spoon into one pound coffee cans, filling two thirds full. Cover with parchment or foil and tie with string. Place on rack in a large kettle and add enough boiling water to reach halfway up the cans. Steam in gently boiling water for three hours. Lift cans from water and remove covering.

Note: This wonderful pudding can be made a few weeks ahead of the holidays and frozen. When cold, remove pudding from cans and freeze in sealed freezer bags. To reheat, bring to room temperature, wrap in foil, then place in the oven for one half hour at 300 degrees. Serve warm with the delicious sauce on the next page.

*Naomi*

# Brown Sugar Sauce for
# Christmas Carrot Pudding   1920s

4 cups water

2 cups brown sugar

2 Tablespoons butter

6-7 Tablespoons flour

4 Tablespoons cider vinegar

2 teaspoons Schilling Pure Vanilla Extract

1 cup raisins, if desired

Mix flour and sugar together. Mix all ingredients except vanilla in saucepan. Cook over medium heat about ten minutes, until clear and thickened. If you wish, add ½ cup raisins 1 or 2 minutes before sauce is done. Remove from heat and add vanilla. Serve quite warm over pudding with a spoonful of whipped cream, if desired. Whipped cream is best with a little sugar and vanilla added.

*Naomi*

# Bessie McCaw Shupe's
# Cottage Pudding   1920s

Cottage pudding was an old-fashioned dessert that, as children, we had a lot. According to Mother, it was much better for us than rich chocolate desserts! Not having rich desserts to compare it to, we really liked it.

½ cup butter

1 cup sugar

2 eggs, well beaten

½ cup milk

2 cups flour

2½ teaspoons baking powder

½ teaspoon real vanilla

Pinch of salt

Cream butter and sugar together. Combine dry ingredients and add alternately with milk to creamed mixture. Bake in oven at 350 degrees, about 30-40 minutes.

While still warm, cut into squares and put each piece in a fruit or soup dish. Poke a hole in the middle of the cake and pour cream over each serving. Enjoy!

*Connie Shupe Plants*

# Bessie McCaw Shupe's
## Sun-Kissed Strawberries   1920s

Strawberries have never tasted better than they do in this recipe! These lovely jewels have captured the sun's rays and are luscious on vanilla ice cream.

Wash and drain 3 quarts strawberries. Boil 2 quarts sugar and 1 quart water in large pan until syrup thickens, at soft ball, 143 degrees, then drop in the berries and let boil gently 3 minutes. Pour on large platter and set in the sun 3 days. Turn the berries every day with a silver fork, then put in bottles or glasses and cover with paraffine. Extra syrup can be bottled for waffles.

*Connie Shupe Plants and Mary Shupe McCarthy*

# Grandmother Mae McCaw's
## Sweet Cherry Pudding   1920s

This was one of Grandmother Mae's favorite recipes and one we looked forward to each summer.

Mix 1 cup flour with ¼ teaspoon salt and 1 scant cup sugar. Add 1 beaten egg and 2 Tablespoons melted butter. Add the juice from 1 cup pitted black cherries and mix. Dissolve 1 teaspoon soda in 1 Tablespoon warm water and add, then add ½ cup nuts and cherries. Bake 40 minutes at 350 degrees. Pour sauce over pudding and return to oven a few minutes.

Make the sauce using 1 cup brown sugar, 1 Tablespoon flour, 2 Tablespoons butter, and 1 cup water. Bring to rolling boil and cook for one minute. Remove from heat and add 1 teaspoon vanilla and pinch of salt. Pour hot over pudding and bake as directed above.

*Jerrianne Powell*

*Cousins Carolyn, on Midget, and Marilyn McCaw joined Naomi for a horseback ride to the Touchet river on an October afternoon in 1944.*

# Ruth McCaw Merrill's
## Scalloped Apples 1920s

This recipe was Ruth's mother Ida's. Quick and easy to make, apple desserts were favorites from fall through winter and into spring. Many large wooden boxes of apples were stored away for eating fresh and for cooking. Having an orchard that produced a thousand boxes of apples every fall meant the women were creative and new recipes were always welcome.

Mix one saltspoonful (1 teaspoon) of cinnamon with half cup sugar. Crumb enough of stale bread to make one pint. Melt two Tablespoons butter and stir into the crumbs. Prepare three pints of chopped apples. Butter a pudding dish and put in a layer of crumbs, half the apples, half the sugar then a layer of crumbs, apples, sugar with crumbs on top. Add half cup of cold water, cover and bake in a moderate oven until done, about 30 minutes. Move near top of oven toward the last to brown the top. Serve hot with cream.

Kay's Note: We liked this served with vanilla ice cream.

*Kay and Dennis Stanley*

# Bessie McCaw Shupe's
# Apple Fruit Roll   1920s

A few years ago our first cousins (all granddaughters and grandsons of Edwin and Ida McCaw) and their spouses enjoyed an afternoon making many gallons of cider on Grandfather's old cider press, then a half mile hike down to the Touchet River. On this bright and sunny October day, we enjoyed a rock-skipping contest, perhaps repeating an event enjoyed many years ago by our parents and grandparents.

Dough:

    2 cups flour

    4 teaspoons baking powder

    ½ teaspoon salt

    2 Tablespoons sugar

    3 Tablespoons shortening

    ¾ cup milk

    1 egg

Syrup:

    1½ cups sugar

    2 cups water

    2-3 Tablespoons butter

Heat the syrup to boiling.

Apples:

    2-3 medium cooking apples, chopped in small pieces.

Make soft dough as for biscuits. Add beaten egg and milk. Roll out ⅓ to ½ inch thick. Spread apples on dough and roll up like a jelly roll. Cut in ¾ inch slices. Place in baking pan and pour the hot syrup over the apples. Sprinkle all with nutmeg. Bake until apples are tender at 350 degrees. Serve warm with cream. Peaches may be used for a delicious change.

*Connie Shupe Plants and Mary Shupe McCarthy*

# Marie McCaw Stanley's
# Springtime Rhubarb Dumplings   1920s

In 1943, one bright morning after a surprise late April snowfall, a mother quail and a dozen tiny chicks came through our garden. The mother quail was walking along some fresh footprints I had just made that were several inches deep. The tiny chicks fell into each footprint and struggled to hop out then fell into the next footprint. With much cheeping they told their mother they were not enjoying this morning walk!

Once the snow has melted, the first fruits appear—rhubarb and strawberries, the real tastes of Springtime!

Boil 1 cup water and 2 cups sugar in a heavy stainless saucepan (not aluminum), with a lid that fits well. Cut 2 slices ⅛ inch thick of an unpeeled orange, then cut in wedges about ⅜ inch wide, rind and all. Add 1 quart thinly sliced rhubarb (¼ - ½ inch). Bring to boil again over medium heat. Make dumplings of 2½ cups biscuit mix, 3 Tablespoons sugar and 1 cup rich milk. Drop by Tablespoonsful into rhubarb mixture. Cover tightly and cook on medium low heat, without peeking, 15 minutes. Serve quite warm with cold cream. The cream and rhubarb are delicious together! This can be refrigerated until cold but our family prefers it warm.

Note: Make sure your biscuit mix is fresh. It ensures the success of this recipe and any other you may have that includes biscuit mix.

*Naomi*

# Bessie McCaw Shupe's
# Deep Dish Apple Crisp   1940s

I remember making apple butter on our big Monarch wood range. It was interesting to cook on this range because you could always find a location for whatever you were making. The area above the fire was very hot, while others were cooler. On the back of the range, the apple butter would cook for hours. Each time we walked by we would stir it with a long-handled wooden spoon and enjoy filling the kitchen with a wonderful spicy apple fragrance. Apple Brown Betty was a popular family dessert long ago and still is an ideal October dessert, now often called Apple Crisp.

Connie's Note: This has been our family's favorite dessert since the 1940s.

    4-6 apples, peeled and sliced

    2 Tablespoons lemon juice

    ¼ cup water

    ½ teaspoon cinnamon

    ⅔ cup sugar

    ¾ cup flour

    ¼ teaspoon salt

    6 Tablespoons butter

Put sliced apples into 9 inch square casserole. Add lemon juice to water and pour over apples. Mix cinnamon with ½ cup sugar and sprinkle over apples. Combine remaining sugar with flour and salt and work in butter with a pastry blender until consistency of coarse corn meal. Cover apples with this mixture and smooth with back of spoon. Bake in 375 degree oven for 40 minutes, or until apples are tender and topping is crisp and lightly browned. Serve warm with ice cream.

*Connie Shupe Plants*

# Mildred Williams Bishop's
# Strawberry Delight   1960s

This was a favorite dessert served to her friends and club members and at Square Dance sessions.

Mix together:

      1½ cups pretzel crumbs

      3 Tablespoons sugar

      ¾ cup melted butter

Put in baking dish, 9 x 12 or 9 x 15, and bake 7 minutes at 400 degrees. Cool.

Mix 1 large package strawberry gelatin with 2 cups boiling water. Add 1 10-ounce package frozen strawberries and 1 can crushed pineapple, drained. Let set to cool.

Mix:

      1 8-ounce package cream cheese, softened

      1 cup sugar

      1 large container Cool Whip topping

Pour on top of cooled crust. Then pour on cooled gelatin. Let set until cold and ready to serve.

*Jane and Bill Williams*

# Ethel McCaw Vernon's Memories

The last day of harvest was always a celebration. We had all the ice cold watermelon and homemade ice cream we could eat.

In the fall it was time to pick the geese for pillows and feather beds. It took all day to pick our flock of geese. We put a long stocking over their heads so we could pick the feathers off.

Maybe the grandchildren would like to hear about the ice house too. In the fall my brothers would take three lumber wagons, with about six horses in each team, and drive forty miles into the Blue Mountains to a lumber mill and bring home loads of sawdust. This was used in packing the winter ice. When the Touchet river froze over to about a twelve-inch thickness, my father and brothers would cut the ice with saws into about 16 by 20 inch slabs. They hauled the ice by sled to the ice house where it was packed between thick layers of sawdust. This preserved the ice for all the next summer. The men certainly appreciated the iced water and lemonade on those hot summer days as they worked in the fields. I can remember my brother Glenn and I taking ice water to the men in the fields in the morning and afternoon.

*From the book* Two Hundred and Fifty Years of McCaws, *A Family History, by Robert H. McCaw*

# Grandfather Edwin's "McCaw Special"
## Orange & Lemon Sherbet 1920s

In the summer the Shady Lawn Creamery in Walla Walla was our favorite place to stop for ice cream and sherbet before the hot drive home to the ranch. Large double scoops of orange sherbet seemed like a bite of heaven after a day of shopping.

This Orange & Lemon Sherbet recipe was developed by Grandfather and soon became our traditional family favorite. We always made it in the old-fashioned freezer, with each child taking turns on the crank. It was always served with saltine crackers, the perfect foil for the tart flavor of the sherbet.

We would bring home a large block of ice from the Shady Lawn Creamery in Walla Walla or the Lockers in Prescott, then my brothers Dennis and Norman would send chunks of ice flying as they used the big ice pick to make the proper chunks for the freezer. Making ice cream surely is the perfect way to spend a Sunday afternoon in the summer.

     8 medium oranges, juice
     8 medium lemons, juice
     1 quart milk
     1 quart whipping cream
     1 quart sugar

Prepare juice from cold oranges and lemons. Remove seeds but do not strain. When juice is ready, put in refrigerator to chill. Combine milk and whipping cream and dissolve sugar in this liquid, stirring very well until completely dissolved. When ready to freeze, quickly mix cream and sugar with juice, stirring until blended. Immediately pour into chilled gallon container and freeze. When firm remove the dasher and replace lid on container. Place additional ice and rock salt around and on top of container. Cover with clean towels or folded newspapers to harden until ready to serve.

Note: Today we use 2 quarts of half and half instead of 1 quart each of milk and cream and find this new recipe even better than the original one.

*Naomi*

# Marie McCaw Stanley's
## Golden Caramel Sauce   1920s

This recipe was tucked away in an old recipe box belonging to my mother and discovered just before Christmas 1992. Rich and buttery, it was irrestible to our friends and grandchildren. They were sure that Santa made it because it tasted so good!

1 cup dark brown sugar, packed

½ cup granulated sugar

⅔ cup whipping cream

¼ cup butter

2 Tablespoons light corn syrup

¼ teaspoon salt

1 teaspoon Schilling Pure Vanilla Extract

Melt butter, add all ingredients except vanilla. Bring to a boil, reduce heat and boil slowly 4 minutes, stirring all the while. Remove from heat, add vanilla, and pour into pint jar. When completely cooled, cover with a lid and store in refrigerator. If covered while hot, sugar crystals may form. Recipe can easily be doubled or tripled. This sauce is out of this world spooned over vanilla ice cream or homemade cream puffs filled with vanilla ice cream. Nice to tuck into gift baskets any time of the year.

*Naomi*

# Caramel Pecan Ice Cream   1990s

One sunny afternoon, I enjoyed creating this ice cream and found it to be rich, different, and delicious.

2 cups room temperature Golden Caramel sauce
2 cups whipping cream
¾ cup pecan halves

Gently blend caramel sauce and whipping cream until well blended and smooth. Add pecans and pour into ice cream freezer and freeze until firm. If ice cream refuses to become firm enough, place in your regular freezer overnight.

*Naomi*

179

# Shupe Family
## Holiday Cranberry Sherbet   1920s

Connie writes: "This cranberry sherbet has always been a tradition in our family. At every Thanksgiving and Christmas dinner this beautiful sherbet accompanied the turkey and was enjoyed by everyone. It was always made in the old wooden ice cream freezer the day before, packed in ice, covered with a gunny sack, and kept in the basement where it was cool. Fifty years later, this adaptation for our freezers of today is still just as delicious."

For two trays sherbet:

    2 cups fresh cranberries, washed and stemmed

    1½ cups water

    1 Tablespoon Knox gelatin (1 envelope equals 1 Tablespoon). Sprinkle over

        2 Tablespoons water and let stand 5 minutes

    2 Tablespoons fresh lemon juice

    1 cup orange juice

    1½ cups sugar

    2 egg whites, beaten to soft peaks, but not too stiff

    1 cup whipping cream, unwhipped (optional)

Add water to berries, cover, and bring to a boil. Simmer 10 minutes, covered. Put through blender to puree. Add sugar to hot syrup and stir until dissolved. Add lemon and orange juice. Pour into 2 ice cube trays and freeze about 1 hour or until mushy. Beat egg whites to soft peaks. Turn frozen mixture into a large bowl and fold in egg whites with a rubber spatula. Turn back into trays and freeze until firm, about 2 hours. Return to bowl and beat on medium mixer speed till thick and smooth. Fold in whipping cream. Return to trays and freeze till hard, 2-3 hours. Serve as an accompaniment to the turkey. It is refreshing, lovely to look at, and delicious.

*Connie Shupe Plants*

# Virgil & Bessie McCaw Shupe's
## Fresh Peach Ice Cream   1930s

This was our father's favorite, and every summer he made it in the old wooden ice cream freezer. How impatiently we waited until the peaches were ripe so we could enjoy this special treat.

    2 cups crushed peaches
    4 cups rich milk (today use half and half)
    ½ lemon, juiced
    1½ cups sugar

Add lemon juice to sugar, then add peaches and milk. Pour into ice cream freezer and enjoy making this wonderful summer treat. Makes about 2 quarts.

*Connie Shupe Plants*


# Marie McCaw Stanley's
## Summer Snowballs   1930s

You will find that children will have great fun making these special treats for friends and family.

Form 1 quart vanilla or chocolate ice cream into balls with ice cream scoop or two spoons. Roll each ball in 2 cups crushed hollow-center peppermint stick candy. Serve topped with chocolate sauce. Aunt Ocea's Velvet Creme Fudge Sauce (on the next page) is marvelous!

# Ocea McCaw's
## Velvet Creme Fudge Sauce   1940s

Aunt Ocea was known in our family for her great cooking. When we visited her family on their ranch near Lowden, she always treated us to new and unusual dishes. Of all the recipes she shared, this is our favorite; it is unbelievably rich and delicious.

1 cube butter, (½ cup)

4½ squares Baker's unsweetened baking chocolate

3 cups sugar

½ teaspoon salt

1 can evaporated whole milk

1 Tablespoon Schilling Pure Vanilla Extract

Slice cube of butter into six or eight pieces, then melt in the top of a double boiler over boiling water. Add cakes of chocolate and stir occasionally until both butter and chocolate are melted. Add one-third of the sugar and one-third of the milk, stirring until well blended. Repeat until all the sugar and milk are added. Add salt. Continue stirring until the sauce is thickened and coats a spoon. This usually takes about 10-12 minutes. Pour into a quart jar or other glass container and refrigerate when cool. This fudge sauce is so rich and thick you may want to stir it a little before serving over ice cream.

Note: This sauce is thick and delicious served as topping for cream puffs filled with vanilla or coffee ice cream. It would also be nice to tuck into gift baskets of treats from your kitchen. If sealing in glass jars, first sterilize both jars and lids in boiling water. And of course, you'll find that you'll want a spoonful now and then!

# Velvet Creme Ice Cream   1990s

After many years of enjoying Ocea McCaw's wonderful dessert sauce (see previous recipe) with my family, I created this ice cream recipe.

2 cups cold Velvet Cream Fudge Sauce
2 cups whipping cream
½ cup broken walnuts

Lightly stir fudge sauce, then measure. Use equal parts fudge sauce and whipping cream, stirring until well blended. This recipe makes one quart, but you can adjust it for any size freezer.

*Naomi*

# Velvet Creme Hot Chocolate
# & Frosty Milk Shakes   1990s

Here are two more creative ways to enjoy Ocea's fudge sauce.

Warm Velvet Creme Fudge Sauce and mix with regular milk by slowly adding milk to the sauce while stirring. Heat until steaming and serve in mugs. The amount of sauce you add will be your choice.

Place several scoops vanilla ice cream in blender. Add cold Velvet Creme Fudge Sauce with whole milk in the amounts you like and blend until creamy.

*Naomi*

*1928-29. Horse drawn sledding scene. Allan Vernon is standing with Dorothy Vernon and Kathleen McCaw. Seated, left to right, are Katherine McCaw, Ethel McCaw Vernon, Jack McCaw, and Alene Vernon.*

184

# Winter

Winter in our valley was a time of quilting bees, when grandmothers, aunts, cousins, and friends gathered in the living room around a large quilting frame to visit and share in the joy of creating something of beauty. And there were always trips to town—to pick up supplies or to attend potluck suppers in the warm, happy atmosphere of the church basement.

Thanksgiving was always a time for a family reunion, and our kitchen overflowed with good cooks who got in one another's way and laughed at the resulting confusion.

But the most exciting time of all was the morning of our first snowfall, when we would wake and see the sun glistening on the snow and dash outside to scoop up an icy handful.

We would sled with our cousins on the hills, then come inside to pop corn over the fire in our old black wire-mesh popper and enjoy it with icy red delicious apples.

Sometimes we would walk in the evening as the snow fell in big, soft flakes. At other times we would have taffy pulls and fudge-making parties.

And then, of course, there was Christmas, with shopping trips to Walla Walla and carols accompanying our search in every store window for special gifts to give our family and friends. Christmas also meant church pageants with costumes to make and songs to learn and little green boxes of hard candy under the church Christmas tree to reward us for a job well done.

# Cookies & Candies

## Cookies

## Candies

# McGrew Mercantile Company

*Dealers In General Merchandise*
Prescott, Wash. March 18, 1928
Mrs. Allen Vernon

| | |
|---|---:|
| 1 Lettuce | $ .10 |
| 2 Bread | .18 |
| 2 Bread | .18 |
| 2 Carrots | .20 |
| Cream of Wheat | .26 |
| Beans | .25 |
| Cheese | .35 |
| Prunes | .30 |
| 2 cans Peas | .50 |
| Shrimp | .23 |
| 1 Lettuce | .10 |
| 2 Tomatoes | .25 |
| | $2.82 |

*Always at your service*
*Pay cash & save*

# Grandmother Ida McCaw's
## Sugar Cookies   1920s

Mother called this cookie Sour Cream Jumbles. Recently my little five-year-old granddaughter Kelly had a happy time with me, testing this recipe from her great, great grandmother.

2 cups sugar

1 cup butter

2 eggs

1 cup sour cream

1 teaspoon soda

3½ cups flour

1 grated fresh nutmeg

1 cup raisins

1 cup coarsely chopped dried apricots

Update:
Cream butter, add sugar, and beat until fluffy. Add beaten eggs and flavoring. Lightly spoon flour into measuring cup, then add baking soda and mix. Add to creamed mixture, making a soft dough. When well blended add raisins and apricots. Drop by spoonful onto greased cookie sheet and bake at 350 degrees for about 15 minutes. This is a soft, creamy textured sugar cookie. Adding the dried apricots makes it wonderful.

*Naomi*

# Marie McCaw Stanley's
# Coconut Kisses   1920s

Easy and quick to make, these are memorable cookies. Recently I talked to a friend from many years ago about this collection of old recipes. He remembered best of all my mother's Coconut Kisses.

    2 egg whites
    1 cup sugar
    2 cups Kellogg's corn flakes
    1 cup moist coconut
    ½ teaspoon Schilling Pure Vanilla Extract

Stiffly beat the egg whites and add the sugar, mixing lightly until fluffy. Add vanilla. Fold in coconut, again mixing gently, then corn flakes, stirring just until blended nicely. Drop by Tablespoonful onto a lightly greased foil-lined cookie sheet, or parchment. Shape each cookie gently, into mounds spaced two inches apart. Bake at 325 degrees 10-15 minutes until lightly browned. Let cookies stand on the cookie sheet about 5 minutes until set, then carefully move to a rack to cool, using a thin metal spatula or pancake turner.

*Naomi*

# Jayne Williams Hall's
# Ginger Cookies   1930s

Jayne's mother-in-law made these crispy, thin ginger cookies and shared her recipe with friends and relatives.

1 cup sugar

½ cup Crisco shortening

½ cup butter

1 cup Brer Rabbit dark molasses

1 cup boiling water mixed with 1 Tablespoon soda

3 cups flour

1 Tablespoon ginger

Cream shortening, add sugar and cream until fluffy. Add molasses to the hot water and soda, stirring until dissolved. Add to creamed mixture. Add ginger to flour, then to above. Stir until well blended. Chill in refrigerator overnight. When ready to bake, set oven at 350 degrees.

Update:
If you like raisins, add 1 cup. Line cookie sheet with parchment or grease cookie sheet, then sprinkle a thin coating of sugar on top. Drop cookie dough by teaspoonful. For thin, crispy cookies flatten each with a glass dipped in sugar. Sprinkle sugar on top if desired. Bake at 350 degrees 10-12 minutes. Let cool in pan for a few minutes then remove to rack to cool.

Note: After taste testing three old, old recipes for Ginger Cookies, my family pronounced these to be the best. The sugar coating on the cookie sheet helps keep the cookies from sticking to the pan. Parchment also works very well.

*Jane and Bill Williams*

# Marie McCaw Stanley's
## Date Bars   1930s

In the early 1930s our father, Lewis Stanley, went deer hunting in the Wallowa Mountains in Oregon, and he would take these favorite cookies in little sacks tied to his belt. When we were children, date bars were always baked at Christmas time. Today they are still a special family treat.

    3 cups dates
    1 cup walnuts
    1 cup flour
    1 cup sugar
    1 teaspoon baking powder
    2 eggs beaten separately
    Pinch of Salt

Rinse, drain and cut dates into small pieces. Break walnuts into large pieces. Put these into the dry ingredients as you cut them. Add beaten egg yolks to this mixture, then the beaten whites. The yolks won't mix much but the whites will make it thin enough to blend if the dates are somewhat moist. You may need to mix with your hand. Use a shallow metal baking pan about 7 x 11 inches.

Before lining pan with heavy waxed paper (or parchment) lightly grease the botton of the pan. This will prevent the waxed paper from sliding around as you place the mixture in by spoonful and press gently into flat shape. Mixture is quite stiff. Bake slowly at 300 degrees and just long enough to make certain the flour is done and surface is very lightly browned, 30-45 minutes. Test for doneness in center with wooden toothpick. Let cool in pan for 15 minutes then remove to rack. Cut into small squares and roll in powdered sugar.

Note: Moist dates are necessary for a successful cookie. Baking in a metal pan is preferred to a glass baking pan because the dough cooks more quickly.

*Kay and Dennis Stanley*

# Grandmother Amanda McCaw Erwin's
# Cry Babies   1930s

On our farms, cookies were enjoyed by everyone in the family but were particularly important to the men, who needed filling snacks during breaks in their work day.

1 cup butter or lard—butter is best

1 cup sugar

1 cup molasses

1 teaspoon soda in 1 cup boiling water

1 egg

1 teaspoon cinnamon

1 teaspoon ginger

4 cups flour

Cream butter or lard, add sugar, and cream until fluffy. Add molasses. Add spices to flour then add to mixture with hot water, alternating and blending after each addition. Add unbeaten egg last. Drop by teaspoonful in a very lightly greased pan. Bake at 350 degrees for ten minutes.

Updated recipe: You may wish to add an additional cup sugar, 2 cups raisins and 2 cups walnuts broken in large pieces. I like to bake the first pan of cookies, taste test, then add the extra ingredients. I prefer lining the cookie sheet with parchment.

*Della Mae Erwin Sanders*

*1920-30. Left to right Dorothy McCaw, Norman, Donald, and John McCaw. All are grandchildren of Robert and Emmaline McCaw.*

# Katherine Holling McCaw's
# Filled Cookies   1930s

Kathleen remembers, "These filled cookies were always made for my dad to take in the mountains when he went deer hunting. Mother would pack them in a coffee can. I have since used the recipe many times, although I don't use the filling any more. I use cookie cutters for all the different holidays and frost the cookies. We now call them 'Cut-Out Holiday Cookies.' Mother received this recipe from Ethel McCaw Vernon."

    2 cups sugar

    1 cup shortening

    2 eggs

    5 ½ cups flour

    2 teaspoons soda

    1 teaspoon cream of tartar

    ½ teaspoon salt

    1 cup milk

    2 teaspoons vanilla

Cream together sugar and shortening. Beat in egg. Sift dry ingredients together and add alternately with the milk and vanilla. After mixing, chill. Roll out and cut in shapes. Bake on lightly greased cookie sheet at 375 degrees for 8-10 minutes until lightly browned.

Filling for Cookies:

    1 cup each ground raisins, dried prunes and walnuts

    1 Tablespoon flour

    ½ cup sugar

    ½ cup water minus 1 Tablespoon

    1 Tablespoon lemon juice

Cook until thick and let cool. Cut out circles of the dough. Place a spoonful of filling on a circle then place another circle on top and press edges together.

*Kathleen McCaw Bergevin*

# McCaw Family
# Peanut Butter Cookies   1930s

Every family has it's favorite peanut butter cookie recipe. This old one is well worth trying.

1 cup brown sugar

1 cup white sugar

1 cup butter

1 cup peanut butter

2 eggs

3 cups flour

2 teaspoons baking soda

⅓ teaspoon salt

1 teaspoon vanilla

Cream butter, add sugars, eggs and vanilla. Add peanut butter and mix well. Add flour and baking soda last. Roll into balls and press with fork. Bake at 400-425 degrees for 10-12 minutes.

*Lois McCaw Ellsaesser*

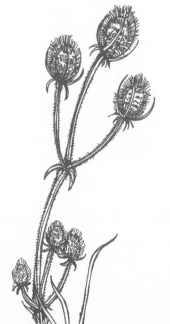

# Ocea McCaw's
## Mincemeat Cookies   1930s

This cookie was always a family favorite for the Christmas holidays.

  1 cup shortening

  ½ cup eggs

  ½ teaspoon salt

  3 Tablespoons water or orange juice

  3½ cups flour

  1½ cups mincemeat

  1½ cups brown sugar

  1 teaspoon soda

  1½ cups chopped nuts

Blend sugar and shortening. Add eggs, then mincemeat and juice. Add sifted dry ingredients. Drop onto lightly greased cookie sheets and bake at 375- 400 degrees for 8-12 minutes.

*Sarita and Bill McCaw*

# Ocea McCaw's
## Oatmeal Refrigerator Cookies  1940s

This was another cookie jar favorite for lunch boxes and sharing with friends as we enjoyed a cup of coffee and coversation.

1 cup shortening

1 cup brown sugar

1 cup white sugar

2 eggs

3 cups quick oats

1½  cups sifted flour

1 teaspoon soda

1 teaspoon salt

½  cup coconut

½  cup chopped nuts

Cream shortening and sugar. Add eggs. Add sifted dry ingredients and oats. Shape into two long or four short rolls. Wrap in waxed paper and chill. Slice and bake at 375 degrees.

*Sarita and Bill McCaw*

# Ocea McCaw's
# Walnut Chocolate Meringue Strips   1950s

When she was the newly elected president of the Washington State Dairy Wives in 1960, Aunt Ocea won First Prize in the Dairy Wives State Cookie Contest with this recipe.

½ cup butter

½ teaspoon vanilla

½ cup sifted flour

1 6-oz. package chocolate bits

1 cup brown sugar

1 egg, separated

¾ cup quick oats

¾ cup chopped nuts

Cream butter. Gradually add ½ cup brown sugar and cream. Mix in vanilla, egg yolk, flour, and rolled oats. Spread in 8 x 8 inch square pan. Beat egg white until stiff. Gradually beat in remaining brown sugar until stiff peaks form. Mix in chocolate and one-half of the nuts. Spread over oatmeal mixture and sprinkle with remaining nuts. Bake at 350 degrees for about 35 minutes. Cut into strips.

*Sarita and Bill McCaw*

# Grandmother Ida McCaw's Diary

## 1910

Grandmother kept diaries nearly all her adult life. These excerpts from those long ago days share her thoughts with us and help us picture ranch life at that time. Ida's husband is Edwin: children are William, Ernest, Marie, Ruth, Bessie, and Dwight.

January  1    I made cookies. *(These are the first words of the diary.)*

4    Churned, baked bread. Children dressed chickens for their school dinner.

8    Baked cookies and bread.

10    Butchered 9 hogs today. 7 degrees above this morning.

13    Ernest and I worked with the lard. Mr. Vernon, the minister, made us a visit in the afternoon and we scorched the lard just a little.

14    Ernest and I worked the lard. Dwight and I made sausage.

26    Willie and I cooked hogs' heads for head cheese.

27    We churned and baked cookies.

28    Ernest and I cooked the backbones and ribs. Baked and housecleaned.

31    Boys resalted the meat.

February 2    Fried doughnuts. (There are weekly entries of "Fried doughnuts and baked bread". Grandmother had to use all that good lard! )

March  16    Baked cookies.

30    Baked pies and fried doughnuts.

## 1911

January  2    Missionary Aid decided to give pigeon dinner and supper Thursday.

5    Bessie and I drove down to Prescott to help with the pigeon and oyster dinner and supper. All stayed for the Prayer Meeting. The Aid made $40. All had lovely time.

March  10    Baked two angel food cakes, 6 loaves bread. With these sent 6 dozen eggs and small box apples for the Aid Window Sale.

|  |  |  |
|---|---|---|
|  | 30 | Husband Ed's birthday, 53 years of age. Baked cake and pies for his birthday dinner. |
| April | 26 | Mother Nature did her washing last night. This morning everything is fresh, bright and beautiful! Had Jim Hill mustard greens for dinner. Excellent! Helped make the wedding cakes for Mrs. Temple. Baked angel food cake for Missionary. |
| June | 9 | Canning Royal Ann cherries. |
|  | 13 | Picked two crates pie cherries. |
|  | 14 | Gathered two buckets pie cherries. Pitted them in afternoon. Canned cherries in evening. |
|  | 29 | We canned beets. |
| July | 4 | All attended the celebration at Prescott. Ruth rode on Liberty car. Aunt Mary rode down to the park with us. Had fine dinner. Nine friends had dinner together. *(Friends were named).* Had lovely time. |
|  | 12 | Ironed today. Gathered beans. Cooking for six hired men. Sewing in afternoon. |
|  | 26 | Made apple dumplings for supper. |
| August | 5 | Making crabapple jelly and marmalade. |
|  | 8 | Everybody hustling trying to get the outfit started to the hill ranch. Everything moved off smoothly as they filed out one team after another until the last took the cook's house and all. And but a few were left to note the change from the hustle and bustle of the morning. |
|  | 10 | Baked biscuits on oil gas stove. Children brought over a bucket of peaches. I gathered cucumbers. Tired. |
|  | 13 | Cooked breakfast in the outdoor cookroom. Baked bread in the old range. Ruth is learning to bake bread and cook. Ruth is 13. |
|  | 18 | Ruth and I took a tramp down through pumpkin patch, gathering beans. Then over to the garden, found squashes large enough to cook, then gathered $\frac{2}{3}$ gunny sack cucumbers, gathered several dozen muskmelons and corn. Ate muskmelon and watermelon and came back to house. |
| September | 1 | Canning peaches. |
|  | 6 | Aunt Polly and Bessie drying apples. Boiled ham in fireless cooker. |
|  | 7 | Canned eleven half gallon peaches in afternoon. |
|  | 19 | Canned two jars grapes. |
| October | 27 | Did baking. Cooked chicken for sandwiches for the Congregational Meeting Friday at church. |

| November 23 | Baking pies and cakes and dressing chickens for Thanksgiving. Marie learning to cut, fit and sew for their dolls. |
|---|---|
| 24 | Thanksgiving. Had good dinner but later in evening. Enjoyed our dinner and supper all together. |
| 28 | Canned 4 cans pumpkin. Ed peeled pumpkins and cut in rings and put up to dry. Ed and Ernest cleaned about half gallon apples seeds from the pomice of the apple they made cider from. Will save seeds for more trees in orchard. |
| December 21 | Children practiced and popped corn for Christmas at Dr. Probst's. |
| 23 | Sewing, baking and preparing for home Christmas tree. |

*Diary held by Mary Louise Shupe McCarthy*

# Grandmother Ida McCaw's
# Sleigh Ride Taffy  1880s

Note to Ida: "This is the recipe we always make candy by and know it is good. Your niece, Linnie."

Grandmother called this taffy Cream Candy. It is really wonderful, for it mellows and changes texture after a few weeks in a covered tin. Then it really is Cream Candy. Children love making this because it needs to be pulled with buttery fingers.

> One pound, (2 cups), white sugar, three Tablespoonsful cider vinegar, one teaspoonful cream of tartar. Add ¼ cup water to moisten the sugar and boil until brittle. Flavor with lemon or pure vanilla, and turn out quickly on buttered plate. When cool, pull until white and cut in squares.

Note: Cook candy to 265 degrees. When warm, and candy is pulled until creamy white, shape into a twisted rope and cut with buttered knife before it hardens. This taffy has a light vinegar taste and is oh, so good!

*Connie Shupe Plants and Mary Shupe McCarthy*

# Aunt Margaret Shupe's
## Candied Orange *&* Grapefruit Peel   1920s

Comment from Connie: "This tangy candy was a family favorite. Our Aunt Margaret made it often."

Peel 2 oranges or 2 small grapefruit and cut the peel into large pieces. Cover with water and cook until tender enough to scrape off white part of peel. Then boil until completely tender. Cool and cut peel into ¼-inch wide strips. Return to kettle and add ⅓ cup water and ⅓ cup sugar. Boil until thick, or until there is practically nothing left but peel. Pour out on waxed paper and sprinkle with sugar. Let cool and dry. Store in air-tight container.

*Connie Shupe Plants*


# Marie McCaw Stanley's Popperjack   1920s

This tastes almost like that Old Time Favorite that comes in a box. Fun for the children and young people to make—and for grandmothers too!

2 quarts popcorn
2 cups brown sugar
2 Tablespoons butter
½ cup water

Place popped popcorn in large container in oven, on warm, while popping the rest. Put butter in saucepan and when melted add sugar and water. Bring to boiling point and boil on medium low for 16 minutes. Pour over hot corn and stir until every kernel is coated. Spoon onto waxed paper and separate into clusters.

*Naomi*

# Marie McCaw Stanley's
## Divinity   1920s

When my brother Dennis was a student at Washington State College in Pullman in 1939-43, we would make this candy and send to him in the mail. His favorite at the time, perhaps it helped him study those long nighttime hours.

> 4 cups sugar
>
> ¾ cup dark Karo corn syrup
>
> ½ cup water
>
> 3 extra-large egg whites
>
> 1 Tablespoon Schilling Pure Vanilla Extract

Place room temperature egg whites in bowl of mixer. Blend sugar, corn syrup, and water in pan. Wipe down sugar crystals on sides of pan with hot damp cloth. On medium heat cook to 248 degrees. Syrup cooks in about 4-5 minutes. Beat egg whites until stiff but not dry. Slowly pour egg whites into the syrup, beating all the while. Add vanilla. Beat candy with stationary electric mixer with flat beater until it is cooling and begins to lose its gloss. Remove beaters and add two cups broken walnuts. Continue beating by hand until candy begins to hold its shape. Drop by teaspoonful onto waxed paper, scooping out each spoonful with another teaspoon. Store in covered container. The flavor mellows after one day and it's the best divinity ever! The dark corn syrup gives a mellow, satisfying richness to the candy.

Note: If you want to make this candy the old-fashioned way, you can beat the egg whites in a large stoneware or ceramic bowl and beat the candy with a large wooden spoon. It is a fun family project with delightful rewards. The modern method is easier. Remember to make all candy when you have a sunny day and you should have great success. The humidity on a rainy day can really make a difference.

*Naomi*

# Grandfather's
# Candy Shop Caramels   1970s

Created by the grandfather of one of our Garden Club members many years ago, when he owned a candy shop, these caramels are surely the best you've ever tasted.

1st Part:

      ½ pound butter (two sticks)

      1 cup whipping cream

      1 cup sugar

      1¾ cups Karo light corn syrup

2nd Part:

      1 cup warmed whipping cream

      2 teaspoons Schilling Pure Vanilla Extract

      1 cup broken walnuts, if desired

In a heavy pan put the first four ingredients, butter first to melt. Stir well and bring to a rolling boil over medium heat. Add cup of warmed cream very slowly while stirring, so the boiling does not stop. Cook to hard ball stage, 247 degrees, gradually lowering the heat and stirring slowly but constantly with a flat-ended spoon. The heat should be on low during the last cooking stage. Remove from heat and add vanilla and pour into a buttered 8 x 8 inch square pan. A metal pan is best. Cool, and when the candy reaches room temperature, cut into 1-inch strips or squares to wrap individually in waxed paper. Store in freezer-type zippered plastic bags in the refrigerator or freezer. When ready to serve, bring to room temperature and cut pieces from the strips. These wonderful caramels can last for several weeks, but once they are discovered by the family, they seldom do!

*Naomi*

# Oregon Trail
# Stories

*The Whitman Mission, founded in 1836 by Doctor Marcus and Narcissa Whitman, served as a Christian, medical, and agricultural mission to the Cayuse Indians. Missionaries, Indians, and Oregon Trail emigrants used the adobe brick buildings until the Whitmans' death in 1847. This painting by David Manuel is located at the Whitman Mission near Walla Walla, Washington. Permission to use this reproduction is granted by the artist.*

# McCaw Family
# Oregon Trail Stories

The pioneers in our family were a literate group of men and women, who understood the historical importance of their experiences. In their later years, several of them wrote lengthy accounts of those early adventures, which bring life on the Oregon Trail and in the pioneer settlements of early-day Oregon and Washington into high relief.

Here, we offer three of those stories. The first, by Sarah B. Findley Radford, tells of the wagon train of 1847. Sarah was the daughter of John and Nancy Findley—born at Fort Vancouver shortly after the family arrived at its destination. That family settled in Linn County in the central Willamette Valley.

The second story is told by Josiah Osborn, who himself crossed the continent and was a survivor of the Whitman Massacre. His is one of the most important first-person accounts of that tragic Indian uprising, which destroyed the mission of Narcissa and Marcus Whitman in the vicinity of present-day Walla Walla, Washington.

The third account is by Belle L. Shirley Green, whose mother, Mary Roundtree Shirley, crossed the plains in 1852 and settled in Polk County, Oregon.

*Harriet Courtney Kees Greer, born in 1851 in Brownsville, Oregon, was a half sister to Sarah B. Findley Radford.*

# A Sketch of Pioneer Days
## Sarah B. Findley Radford

*Sarah B. Findley Radford was a niece of our great grandmother Sarah,
wife of William McCaw.*

*In Honor of My Parents and Grandparents, Pioneers of Oregon.
Dedicated to my children and grandchildren, in whose love I repose.*

In taking up the pen, I see, looming on the horizon of my mind, a long train of canvas-covered wagons, slowly wending its way, bearing precious living freight of brave souls, amid danger, hardships and privation, to face the perils of an unknown land.

On they come, o'er desert and plain....On over turbulent streams and rugged mountains to the land of The West.

Elias Buell [Mrs. Findley's maternal grandfather] was born July 20, 1797, in the town of Benton, New York, Welsh parentage. Sarah Hammond [her maternal grandmother] was born January 2, 1780, in the town of Liberty, Frederic County, Maryland. Elias Buell married Sarah Hammond, Allensville, Indiana, October 19, 1819. They were the parents of nine children, the two eldest died in infancy.

The Buells emigrated from Indiana to Louisa County, Iowa. There five daughters and a son were born. The eldest living was born in Switzerland County, Indiana. My mother's birth occurred November 12, 1826, in Louisa county, Iowa. Her name was Caroline Buell. In 1846, the Findleys, John and Nancy and sons, went to St. Joseph, Missouri, where emigrants assembled in readiness for the long journey to Oregon.

There they became acquainted, during the winter, with the Buell family and on May 4, 1847, James L. Findley and Caroline Buell were wed.

In the course of time, the train of 1847, the original of the mental picture drawn in the opening of this record, bid a sad farewell to relatives and friends, and swung westward into the unknown.

From St. Joseph, they rolled down the Missouri river to Independence, the starting point. Memory recalls a few of the noted points I heard my parents mention in the early times; but I had ever wished for more information regarding the routes and distance from the starting point to the Pacific, being a native daughter of the Oregon Country. However, I escaped a tedious and tiresome journey; and which is of far more moment, the danger connected therewith.

The following [example of that danger] was related to me by my mother:

In the sunshine of a summer day, as the train came peacefully moving along, Indians were seen collecting on the low ridges farther on....The train halted, and was corraled, and preparations of defense begun by constructing a barricade of feather beds, which were fastened to the inside wagon wheels. It had been said, an arrowhead could not penetrate a feather bed.

The men thus busily engaged, had not time to replenish their supply of ammunition; but women with ladles and bullet molds were attending to that. There were no Winchester rifles at that time. But, why did the red men delay? And why was there no attack? The watchful warriors on the uplands decided discretion [was] the better part of valor, and our train, unmolested, moved on. On through heat, and dust, that could hardly be endured: the dust had been caused by previous travel.

In many places wood, water and grass were scarce, and where there was no fuel, food was cooked over a fire of buffalo chips.

Where neither wood nor water prevailed the deceptive mirages were sometimes seen. Memory recalls a remarkable one. In the late afternoon, as the train came rolling along, there appeared in the distance a line of timber, large and beautiful trees, stretching across the country. Timber indicated water, also. The delightful scene continued for a time, as the weary pilgrims, with happy anticipation, came moving toward it, then finally faded away. "Twas only an optical illusion."

While on the journey, they were accompanied for a few days by Brigham Young and his people from Nauvoo, Illinois, their destination being the Great Salt Lake. The prophet endeavored to persuade the immigrants to Oregon to settle there! But they were bound for Oregon.

They reached the Platte some twenty miles below what is now Grand Island. One night, when encamped on that river, a terrific storm was experienced. Keen flashes of lightning rent the air, accompanied by peal after peal of reverberating report, and a torrent of rain fell.

"Within a tent, during the storm, were nurses wading around a bedside placed upon chairs, ministering to the mother and new-born babe. The little maid, whose birth occurred that night on the Platte, a real, though tender, pioneer of Old Oregon Country, became, in the course of time, an early settler of eastern Washington Territory; and is, at the present time, an estimable resident in a thriving town of that state. From Grand Island, the trail turned up the Platte to its forks, some four hundred and thirty-five miles. The trail

212

five hundred and thirteen miles from the starting point, turned abruptly to the North Fork, thence rolled on six hundred and sixty-seven miles to Fort Laramie. This fort was the last post on the eastern side of the towering Rockies.

From Fort Laramie, the road wiggled along the course of the Platte, until it reached a point eight hundred and seven miles from Independence, then it abandoned the Platte, and swung over into the valley of the Sweetwater.

One of the famous features of the road, then and now, is Independence Rock, eight hundred and thirty-eight miles from Independence. Encamped one evening within sight of the rock, my parents and others, supposing the distance to be about eight miles, decided to walk out to it. Leaving their campfire early in the evening they strolled on and on; but reached there finally, at 2:00 AM, having tramped nearly all the night. This rock is a sort of crude register on whose face may still be traced the names of numbers of the pioneers, guides, adventurers and scouts who passed that way.

Up the Sweetwater, the pioneers passed the foot of Big-Horn Mountains, and the Devil's Gate, and thence through the South Pass, discovered by Etienne Provost.

There, nine hundred and forty-seven miles from the Missouri river's western bank, they started down the Pacific slope of the Great Divide. They crossed Green river and rested and purchased supplies at Fort Bridger, almost half way between the Missouri and the Pacific. Following the Bear river, the emigrants dropped down to Soda Springs on the Big Bend, one thousand two hundred and sixty-six miles from the starting point. When crossing a swollen stream, my parents had a narrow escape from drowning. The teams getting off the bar were drifting into deep water; in fact, the lead oxen were swimming when father plunged into the river, swam to their heads, and taking them by the horns, turned them around and up stream, thus averting a sad accident.

Another thrilling event was that of a stampede. The oxen were being yoked, preparatory to leaving camp, but all were free, except my father's teams; the wheelers [were] hooked to [the] wagon tongue and the leaders with chains adjusted, stood awaiting the train to get in line. Mother, sole occupant of the wagon, sat waiting also.

The plodding cattle, which were so patient when under the yoke, became frightened, and the herd ran; father's teams, and, of course, mother and wagon, along with them. I will bring this otherwise long story short, by recording there was nobody hurt, and but little damage but mother was much frightened.

At one thousand two hundred and eighty-eight miles from Independence, they reached Fort Hall, established by Nathaniel J. Wyeth, in 1834, on [the] Snake river....From Fort Hall, the train of 1847 rolled on down the Snake river, until reaching its noted tributary, the Boise river, and there the seams of wagon boxes were caulked to prevent leakage, and used as boats, two being lashed together side by side.

All, with their belongings, were ferried over to the opposite bank of Snake river, and with another obstruction overcome, they continued on down the river a day's drive, then across the country eight miles to the Malheur river, and then, five miles from its conjunction with [the] Snake river, they crossed the Malheur, and rolled on to Burnt river, then up that stream some distance to where the old emigrant road led up a steep and long bunchgrass hillside, on over a divide and down to South Powder river, thence to North Powder, and over a sagebrush plain, to dip down into Grand Ronde valley and on to the Blue Mountains. On the mountains they were met by a messenger from Dr. Marcus Whitman at Waiilatpu Mission on the Walla Walla river, six miles west of where stands Walla Walla City of the present day.

An Indian, riding a white horse, approached the captain of the train, and gave him a letter, containing the request to those on the mountain, to push on, if possible, down the Columbia river.

Leaving the mountain, they went rambling on, and camped on Umatilla river, where later stood Fort Henrietta, the rendezvous of a company of volunteers during the Indian uprising in 1855 or 1856, where now stands the flourishing town of Echo.

From Umatilla they came wending their way to lively meandering Butter Creek, next door neighbor to the girlhood home of the humble writer. The name originated through the stealing of a keg of butter from the camp of the soldiers, so I heard related in reminiscence of other days.

In this simple record, for those who may scan these lines, and to you, dear children, and to all whom they may concern: I'm endeavoring to bring our loved pioneers on the last lap of their tedious and tiresome journey, and they are now nearing The Dalles.

Having arrived at The Dalles, on Oregon's famous river, the mighty Columbia, their mode of travel changed. As there was nothing but an Indian trail down the river, these pioneers were compelled to board the rafts ere reaching their destination. There were men to bring the teams along the trail, and my father, who was one of the number, became stricken with mountain (typhoid) fever, and was borne, seriously ill, on to the Fort. There he lingered until December 23, 1847, and passed to the Great Beyond. There were others whose deaths occurred during the winter of 1847-48. When the Pioneer Cemetery was plotted their remains were exhumed and reinterred. Those of my father were petrified; and as the body rests beneath the sod, the form and features are as they were when the Spirit took its flight from the clay, nearly 80 years ago.

But I must turn from these sad reflections, and write for the benefit of those who have no records to which they can refer, taking it for granted that such may sometimes be scanning these lines.

Fort Vancouver, Oregon Country. The first clergyman of the Church of England, or Protestant Episcopal Church, was Reverend Herbert Beaver, who arrived at Vancouver in 1836 to serve as chaplain of the Hudson's Bay Company.

The first school in Oregon Territory was at the Hudson's Bay Company, Fort Vancouver, and at the request of Dr. John McLoughlin, Chief Factor, was taught by John Ball, a native of New Hampshire, but a graduate of Dartmouth College. He came to that place with Captain N. J. Wyeth in 1832, and began the school in November of that year. Among his pupils of mixed blood were three who became very well known in later years, William C. McKay, M.D., David McLoughlin, youngest son of Dr. John McLoughlin, and Ranald McDonald, son of Archibald McDonald, a cousin of Dr. William C. McKay.

When I was born at Fort Vancouver, March 28, 1848, Oregon was not known as a territory, although the provisional government, organized May 2, 1843, was in existence. The principal towns of Oregon were Oregon City, Salem, and Astoria.

Leaving Fort Vancouver in the summer of 1848, my grandparents moved to the Willamette valley. Grandfather, on my father's side (a stockman), sought pasture land in Linn county, and took a donation land claim. A man and wife could each take three hundred and twenty acres; total, six hundred and forty acres. Whereas, the unmarried man was allowed but three hundred and twenty.

My maternal grandparents and family, my widowed mother and baby included, found a favorable location in Polk county. On the arrival of the early immigration to Oregon, they found a country hardly touched by man. Great timber resources and untouched, productive valleys; and game, also plentiful, added much to the joy of living.

My grandfather of Polk county was a miller. He and grandmother helped themselves to a portion of Uncle Sam's generous donation. It was located at the upper end of a pretty little valley, with a background of mountains, forest and streams. One of the last named left its mountain retreat and came meandering on through the claim. Back in the timber a half mile from the dwelling, a lumber mill was built, and in due time a flour mill was constructed down on the farm.

Mother made her home with her parents, but took trips occasionally to Linn county; and it was while visiting there, she became acquainted with John R. Courtney, who came with his parents from Illinois to Oregon in 1845. In course of time, they married. The wedding was solemnized on March 26, 1849. Reverend William Helm officiating.

John Courtney, the father of John R., filed on the first Donation Claim which was taken south of the Calapooia river in Linn county. Father Courtney and two eldest sons felled timber, erected a big log house with puncheon floor, home-made furniture and a fireplace of stones gathered from the hillside—a humble home, lighted by candles and firelight glow from the chimney at the end, where around its hearthstone a happy family gathered. A few short years passed, and Mr. Courtney, when walking with a friend in the timber, near Oregon City, was crushed to death by a burning tree that fell on him as they were passing.

When the pioneers poured into Linn County, those from the prairies of Illinois and Iowa settled near the timber, and the prairie was slower in being settled. In these humble cabin homes dwelt a happy, hospitable people, whose latch-strings were always out to those who had borne the heat of the day, and "the toils of the road" together to this land to which they came.

I will now turn back the scroll of time, and record something of that which they found [in Oregon].

Indians had kept the underbrush burned to afford a hunting ground; so timbered regions were open. Ah! These delectable mountains; the tumbled range of the Calapooia (spurs of the Cascade Mountains). Its matchless woods, that in springtime are interspersed with flowering wild currant, the bloom of dogwood, wild cherry and crabapple trees, and in the sylvan shade, soft mosses and wildflowers grow. Over fallen timber luxuriant vines ran, that in season bore the luscious Oregon wild blackberry, of which delicious pies and cobblers were made. The foregoing would have been a place for an artist with his brush, and it was the hunter's paradise, also.

Among the giant pine and towering firs could be heard the hoot of grouse, the drumming of pheasant, and the call of the mother quail to her brood beneath the alders. If the hunter cared naught for fried pheasant for breakfast, he could step to a silvery stream where trout leaped to catch the fly.

After Mr. Courtney's death, ere my parents had taken a donation claim, they lived with the widowed mother, and father Courtney, and a brother ran a sawmill.

With lumber available, better dwellings were built, and many log cabins were abandoned; school and church houses were erected, which were greatly needed, as children were out of school, and Divine services were being held in the homes of the settlers. Pioneers began to settle on the prairie, which prompted my parents to take a claim.

Two and a half or three miles southwest of Brownsville was a beautiful grove of oak, on a wide prairie, in a valley of unsurpassed beauty. There where our feathered neighbors, the little meadowlarks trilled their sweet notes, a part of my childhood days were spent. Taking a motor trip with some friends a few weeks ago from Portland, to once more gaze upon these old places, and the changing scenes of time, there were many pleasant memories intermingled with sadness. The grove, much larger grown, still stands, an old landmark on the John R. Courtney Donation Land Claim.

My father began farming, as did those around the foothills, with nothing but a walking plow and sickle to harvest the grain. I remember seeing my father walking slowly over the field, taking handfuls of seed from a sack slung around his waist and flinging them broadcast. When the field became green with growing grain, it was extremely alluring to the wild geese, and we children, little brother, sister and myself went every day to rout them; which went very much against the geese, (not the grain), in that case. The grain was harvested, cutting it by hand with a sickle, bundling it with a wooden rake and tying the bundles with grain ropes, just wisps of the grain taken up and twisted, if you know what I mean; then hauled to the threshing floor, which was a cleared space, around a big oak tree. The sheaves were placed around the circle, and horses were ridden over them until the grain was tramped out; then pitchforks were used to remove the straw, the grain taken up and put through a fanning mill to separate the chaff, and then taken to the grist-mill.

While our physical nature was being provided with food, the spiritual was not neglected; and the seed sown resulted in a good setting. There were Presbyterian, Methodists, and Baptists. A few heralds on the Halls of Zion were Reverend Wilson Blain of Union Point, Linn county; Professor Thompson of the United Presbyterian Church; Reverend Joseph McKinney and wife, who came to the Oregon Country as missionaries in 1840, and were Methodists; Reverend Joab Powell, Baptist, had appointments all over the valley, and was familiarly known as "Uncle Joab." People from far and near traveled miles to hear him speak. And he would say in new districts, when closing services: "All those who wish Joab to come back and talk to them, will now make it known by coming forward and giving me their hands." And they assuredly did.

The death of my grandfather of Linn county occurred April 26, 1858, following that of his son Milton Findley, who passed away in the year 1854.

My grandparents were Presbyterians. Father Courtney's people, also, were of that denomination. My mother, her parents and relatives of Polk county, were members of the Methodist Episcopal church.

Two years after my grandfather's death, my parents disposed of their land and father Courtney, after leaving mother and children to spend the time during his absence with relatives in Polk county, gathered his stock which had been accumulated, and with men and pack animals, bid goodbye to relatives and friends, and started to the bunchgrass range, also the land of sagebrush and sand. Where stands the city of Eugene, they turned their course to cross the mountains where, at that time, there were no roads, and they had to trust to their discernment of direction. All went well for a time, until discovering they were lost. Getting out of provisions, they subsisted upon beef until they found their way out. And that was over the snow around the foot of the South sister, in the Cascade range. They finally reached Umatilla, and finding a location, father returned, but, too late to take us that year, and wintered again in the valley.

A number of the young persons who came across the plains with this company returned to the east and located near their parents. And those who went to Wisconsin

decided, after a few years, to return to Oregon; and while en route to Oregon by the way of California, were lost in the wreck of the ill-fated *Brother Jonathan*, twelve miles from Crescent City, on July 30, 1865. This steamship was endeavoring, when in a storm, to make a port; but shortly after turning around towards Crescent City, struck a reef which was not discovered until too late.

When the sad message reached our folks grandfather hastened to Crescent City and by awaiting the return of bodies borne in by the tide, recovered his daughter, and son in law and had them interred in a cemetery at Crescent City. The bodies of their four children were never found. Poor grief-stricken grandfather never became reconciled to the loss and six years later passed on to meet them where sorrow and parting are no more. He was seventy-four years of age then. My grandmother passed to the beyond, aged 85 years. My father's mother died January 6, 1896, at the age of 93 years, one month and twenty-three days. My mother followed April 27, 1897, aged 71 years, four months and fifteen days. Father Courtney died in 1903 or 1904.

My father had been successful in business, a benefactor to the community in which he lived, and one of the founders of Willamette University in Salem.

We bid those loved ones, who have since passed on to the "West beyond the West", those whose blood flows in our veins, a sad, and a long farewell. My mother was again to traverse a part of the long trail she had traveled previously. Memory recalls each whom we have lost, but 'tis only for a while. And in closing these lines, I am giving fond affection to dear children and friends.

*Nancy Osborn Kees Jacobs was the daughter of Josiah Osborn and a survivor of the Whitman Massacre.*

# Letter From Oregon
## Josiah Osborn

*Oregon, April 7th 1848, Printed in Oquawka, Illinois* Spectator, *1848.*

*Our great grandmother Sarah Findley McCaw was an aunt to Margaret Findley,*
*wife of Josiah Osborn.*

Dear Brother and Sister:...After a long silence I take my pen in hand to write you a few lines to inform you that some of us still remain on this side of the grave; and give you some information of the country, and our troubles since we left the States. I have waited a long time until I could have something worth writing about.

When we parted with you, we took our journey for Oregon, and had a very pleasant trip, but traveled very slowly. When we reached the Umatilly river we turned and went to Dr. Whitman's, where we spent the winter. We had a very pleasant winter. On the first of March, 1846, we started for the Wallamette Valley, and in thirteen days we had completed our boat, and then started down the Columbia, and arrived at Oregon city on the 24th of April. Here we spent the summer, and in the fall moved up the Wallamette to the Methodist Institute, and spent the fall and winter. In the spring of '47 we went to our claim on the Califosea, and thought we were done moving.

Dr. Whitman came down and wanted me to undertake to build two mills for the Mission—and not being satisfied when doing well, I consented to go and spend two years in working for the Mission. On the last of September, we started for Oregon City. About the first of October we took water at the City, with six Walla Walla Indians, for the Falls (Celilo Falls, on the Columbia river), which we reached on the 5th. Next day we saw the dust rise from a caravan coming from the States; I started to meet them, and the first persons I met were John and Nancy Findley, driving the loose cattle; after passing a few words with them I went on and met the wagons. The first was driven by William McCaw. In this wagon I found one whom I had never expected to see again in this world...here was aunt Jane Findley, sitting in the wagon, almost worn out with traveling. She was surrounded with a host of little children...three of Levi Russell's, four of Dunlap's and one of McCaw's.(Mary Jane)...all dependent upon their grandmother to be taken care of...a burden for the stoutest person. (Aunt Jane was 66 years old). Then up rode James L. Findley and his wife, in good health, then came Alexander Findley, John Dunlap and Milton; Dunlap had been sick for several days. This was a very solemn meeting of friends. After bracing myself up as well as I could, I led this little caravan on to my family. The caravan soon passed on to camp, but John and Nancy Findley remained and took tea with us, and in the evening we went with them to the camp.

A day or two afterwards we met another caravan in which were David Findley and his family, they had buried their youngest child three days before. Putman had taken the road to the Cascades...thus our friends were scattered along the road, trying to find the Wallamette Valley. We now hired another crew of Indians to take us to Fort Walla-Walla up the Columbia river. After bidding farewell to our friends, we put our goods aboard of a small boat, dug out of a white cedar, and started with four Indians. With hard labor we got about half way through the Big Falls, and camped among the rocks by the water's edge. In the morning we got Indians to carry some of our goods about to the upper end of the Falls. We then went aboard and proceeded on our way to Dechutes' Falls, and camped. Next morning, made our portage, and went on...so made our way up the river, (Columbia) passing through many dangers, not only by the river, but by being almost without food, except as we bought from the Indians along the river. We ran out of provisions, and had to buy dried salmon. Our children suffered very much with the cold. In ten days after leaving the Falls we arrived at Fort Walla Walla.

On Sabbath morning the team came for us, with provision, and on Monday noon we reached the Mission, where the Doctor and Mrs. Whitman, and Mr. Andrew Rogers, met us with great friendship. We found Mr. Rogers very unwell, but on the mend. Several families had stopped here for the winter. The Cayuse Indians were dying very fast with the measles and dysentery. In about two weeks the Doctor's family took them,(measles) and as we lived in an adjoining room, Margaret (Mrs. Osborn) was taken down on the 8th of November, and being in delicate situation the disease went very hard with her, and resulted in the death of the child, which was born on the 14th and was buried next day. When it was taken to the grave, Salvijane was taken down, as we supposed with the measles, and never rose again; in five or six days she became speechless and died on the 9th day after she was taken. Our other children, John Law, A. Rogers and Nancy Anna were all taken sick, but Nancy was able to be about all the time. I was also sick for several days.

In the last company (wagon train) there was a half-breed came to the Doctor's and hired to work through the winter. One day he was at work for Indian named Tamsicky, harrowing in wheat and told him that the Doctor and Mrs. Whitman were scattering poison into the air, and would kill them all off...that he was not working for him, but for the Doctor...that he (the Doctor) knew they would all die and he would get their wheat and all they had. He then proposed that if they would agree to it, he would help them to kill the Doctor and his wife, and all the Americans in their country. As they had a disposition to murder, and wanted satisfaction for the loss of women and children, it was no difficult matter to incite them against the Americans.

On the 29th day of November the Indians convened for the purpose, apparently of burying their dead, and continued coming in nearly all day. About one or two o'clock, Margaret got up and went into the parlor to see the sick children... the first she had walked for three weeks. The Doctor and his wife were in the room, and an Indian came to the door and spoke to the Doctor, who went out into the kitchen. Mrs. Whitman now bolted the door, and firing soon commenced. Kimble, Camfield and Huffman were dressing a beef in the yard, Sanders was in the school room, and the other men were at their work. I was in my room, on the bed. The Indians commenced on all at nearly the same moment. They killed the Dr. and wounded the three men at the beef, and killed a young man in the room with the Doctor and Mr. Gillyean the tailor. Margaret came back into our own room...I asked her what was the matter...she answered that the Indians had risen to kill us. A constant firing was now kept up. Sanders was killed in attempting to get to his family...Kimble got into the house with his arm broke, and got up stairs with the children. Mrs. Whitman being informed that her husband was not yet dead, with the assistance of another woman she dragged him into the parlor. She was shot in the breast, and Mr. Rodgers got her up stairs, and he, by presenting a gun at the head of the stairs kept the Indians down, but about sunset they promised that if Mr. R. and the rest would come down and go to the house where the emigrants were, they would not kill any more. Mr. R., with the assistance of an Indian, got Mrs. Whitman down, but no sooner had they got outside of the house than the Indians fired several balls into Mrs. Whitman. They shot Mr. Rogers three times, and left him to die. His last words were "Come Lord Jesus! Sweet Jesus". A few minutes before this last occurrence, I had lifted up the floor and we got under, with our three children, and put the boards back in their place. We lay there listening to the firing—the screams of women and children—the groans of the dying—not knowing how soon our turn would come. We were, however, not discovered.

When it had become dark, and all was quiet, we concluded to leave everything, take our children and start for the Fort (Walla Walla), which was twenty-five miles distant, knowing that if we remained until morning, death would be our portion. Taking John Law on my back, and A. Rogers in my arms, we started. This night we traveled only two miles. We hid in the brush, and then spent another mournful day in the Indian country. When night came, finding that Margaret was unable to travel, I took John Law on my back and started for Walla Walla yet twenty miles distant. When I had arrived within six miles of the Fort, I laid down in the wet grass till morning. About 9 0'clock I reached the Fort where

223

*This photograph by Ted Nelson shows the present-day Oregon Trail at the Whitman Mission.*

Mr. McBean met me, and told me that he had reported me among the dead. He gave me about a half pint of tea, and two small biscuits. When we had got warm, I asked for assistance to bring in my family, but was unable to procure any. During the day Mr. Stanley came up from Fort Collville with two horses which he offered me. At night, we got a little more to eat, and an Indian being hired to go with me, I prepared for a start. Mr. McBean said I must go to the Bishop on the Umatilla. I refused, but he said I must, for if I came back we could not have a mouthful of food. I asked him for some bread to carry to my family, for they had had nothing but a little cold mush since Monday. He gave me none, but Mr. Stanley gave me some bread, sugar, tea and salt, and gave John Law a pair of socks and a fine silk handkerchief.

The Priest gave me a letter to the Bishop. All being ready we started—the Indians leading the way, and made all haste to get back to my wife and children. When we came near we commenced hunting but could not find them, owing to the dark. We gave up the search until daylight, soon after we found them, almost perished with hunger and thirst.

224

The Indian got water, and I gave them bread—and in about ten minutes we began to get ready to start—being so near the Indians that had committed the murder, our guide was anxious to return. We started to go by the (Hudson's Bay) Company's Farm, and had not got more than two miles, where we got off at a creek, before we saw an Indian coming toward us—he came up with speed and spoke very friendly to me, but told my Indian that he would kill me, and put his hand on his pistol—My Indian asked him if he was an old woman, that he would kill an old man that was sick, with a sick wife and children? After they talked for some time, he replied that as he never had shed blood, he would not—but said tell him to hurry and be gone, for the murderers will follow and kill him before he gets to the Umatilla. My Indian told me to hurry—we started and the Indian followed close behind for some distance and then left, and we soon got to the farm where we were to change horses. We were directed to stop here till night, but the Frenchman would not let us stay, for he said the Indians would be there before night. Here was the first fire that Margaret and two of the children had seen since Monday. We warmed a few minutes and started as though we would go to the Bishop's. When we were out of sight we turned and thought we would risk going to the Fort. We went on as fast as we could, but soon after dark Margaret gave out, and had to be tied to the Indian's back, but we got to the Fort about 10 o'clock. Mr. McBean helped us into an empty room, and we soon had a fire. We had hardly got warm before McBean came to me and wanted me to leave my family with him and go down to the (Willamette) Valley by myself, but I refused to leave the Fort (Walla Walla) and would not go—but God fed us here until Mr. Ogden came up from Fort Vancouver, and brought the women and children here. (Peter Skeene Ogden ransomed the captive survivors from the Whitman Mission, from the Indians. We had to spend one month among Roman Catholics and Indians, and fed for some time on meat—and having but little bread—we helped to eat one horse, which gave my wife the dysentery.

Mr. Ogden, one of the principal Agents of the Hudson's Bay Company took us down to Oregon City. After we got to the City, John Law died and was buried in the same grave with J. Alexander Findley. I can say but little more about the massacre; we may say, however, that it was nothing but the hand of Almighty God, that delivered us out of the hands of these cruel savages.

The climate of Oregon is pleasant and healthy. Wheat is good here, so are vegetables. Father Courtney was killed by the falling of a tree. Putman lost his wife with the camp fever. There is a call here for all kinds of machinery. I am now building a saw and grist mill for Rees and Cottle. Jane and Lydia were married about new-years. Jane lost her husband this month—the rest are well.

*Ezekiel Allen Shirley and Mary "Polly" Turner Roundtree Shirley, parents of Belle Shirley Green.*

# The Wagon Train of 1852
## Belle L. Shirley Green

*Belle Shirley Green and grandmother Ida Murphy McCaw were first cousins. Their mothers, Mary (Polly) Roundtree and Elizabeth (Betsy) Roundtree Murphy were young women in their twenties when they journeyed over the Oregon Trail with their parents, Turner Richardson and Mary Ferguson Roundtree, and their five brothers. Belle Shirley Green married and lived in the Pullman, Washington area.*

*This document is in the original form as received in January, 1994, from Jim and Maryly Dahlquist. The Dahlquist collection is now located at the Washington State University Library, Pullman, Washington.*

This story of my mother's trip across the plains was commenced nearly sixty years ago by Mary Roundtree Shirley, my mother. I have many notes she had, some written with pen and ink, others with pencil, so faded and rubbed out that they were almost impossible to read. She used to tell me so much about the trip and things she did, and the happenings of the time.

When I was a child people used to come and stay for a few days to visit, who had crossed the plains in the same company, as I remember the trip across was all they talked about.

My mother and I had collected all the history we possibly could of several generations of our family. I have clippings and old letters yellow with age, and memory of the things mother told to me. I give to you this narrative of the Elijah B. Davidson and Murphy train that left Knox County, Illinois, in April, 1852, for the Oregon.

In writing this narrative I have thought of that verse by Longfellow:

*Deeds of great men all remind us*
*We can make our lives sublime,*
*And departing leave behind us,*
*Footprints on the sands of time."*

*Signed: Belle L. Shirley Green*

## April 1852

My father was born in Kentucky in 1826. He crossed the plains in 1851. He settled on a donation claim in Polk County, Oregon Territory. My mother was born in Hart County, Kentucky, in 1826. Some of the relations had been planning for some time to go to Oregon, most all the neighborhood were talking of the opportunities for a man who had the courage to face the dangers of the long trail, the persistence to make a home for himself and his family and the foresight to see the future of the Pacific Coast.

A married man was entitled to a donation claim of 640 acres. The unmarried man could have a claim of 320 acres for his home. Such wealth to be obtained turned every conversation into a desire on the part of men and women to move westward; between home and their goal lay two thousand miles of unsettled, unsurveyed ground. But as neighbors began to plan the long journey they combined into groups, elected one of themselves captain, and made laws by which they agreed to abide. There was much planning and work to be done, wagon beds were built, with the thought of the high water. Hickory for the wagons was plentiful. Young oxen [had] to be trained to be worked with new yokes, which had to be cut, trimmed and bowed, and water tight boxes and chests built to store linen, linsey-woolsey blankets, quilts, homespun sheeting, pillows and feather beds.

## Departure

All winter the wheels had been spinning, loomweaving linen towels, table cloths, counterpanes, bed clothing, homespun sheets, linsey-woolsey, yarn for stockings for women and girls, sox for men and boys, mittens, and gloves. Into boxes were packed the results of the winter's spinning and weaving for the trip.

The day for departure had come. The captain called the roll of his party. They were mostly related to each other, a family affair. They said goodbye, and early in April of 1852 the great trek westward had begun. The food supply for the trip had been packed in tight boxes. It consisted of dried peaches, apples, dried corn and beans, coffee in toe sacks, tea, spices, sugar, flour, salt, bacon, salt pork, cheese, chewing tobacco, hard-tack, crackers, a good supply of heavy leather shoes, homemade for women and children, and laced with buck-strings very strong and durable. I have heard emigrants say that they wore out a pair of shoes in about three hundred miles of walking and travel. Then the men and boys must have a good supply of good heavy leather homemade boots. Six or seven months of hard wear would require quite a few extra pair of boots and shoes for each member of the family. The arsenal for the train consisted of old fashioned muzzle-loading guns, and plenty of powder and bullets with bullet molds for making more when needed.

## The School Wagon of 1852

My grandfather Roundtree had fitted up an ox team and wagon for his daughter, Polly Roundtree, my mother, who was going on this trip across the plains with her sister, Betsy Murphy and her husband William Murphy, with their family of growing children to help with the cooking....These sisters also had three brothers in the company, Doctor James H. Roundtree, Parry O. Roundtree, and Andrew Roundtree. All settled in Lewis County, Washington Territory, in 1852.

Martin Roundtree was sheriff of Lewis County in the early Territorial days. Turner R. Roundtree, my grandfather, served under the gallant Harrison in the war of 1812 and was in the battle when the famous Indian Chief Tecumseh was killed.

Grandfather was anxious about the children of the train, not being in school for six or more months. That was why he wanted his daughter who had been teaching in Illinois to go with her sister and teach the children, so her wagon came to be called the school wagon of the Murphy and Elijah B. Davidson train of 1852.

Grandfather had...boxes and chests made for my mother that fitted in the wagon box tightly so not to lose any space. When ready to pack the boxes and chests for the long trip, mother put in the things she would want in her new home in Oregon. She had beautiful quilts, counterpanes, linen table clothes, towels and sheets she had woven, also she had carded the wool and spun it and woven blankets for beds, linsey-woolsey for dress goods or men's shirts. She had both linen and woolen bolts of yardage and yarn for stockings. All this wool came from her father's flock of sheep in Illinois. At first this school wagon was supposed to be for the children of the kinfolks in the company, but later it came to be for all the children. Each child would study and recite each day. She had in the wagon at one time as many as she could conveniently seat on the fitted and packed boxes. When this group had recited their lessons for the day, she took the smaller children by the hand and leaning over the side of the wagon helped them out while the wagon rolled along. The...larger children could get out without help. Some of the larger girls, mostly her nieces, she taught to sew, darn, and knit. The larger boys had horses to ride and drove the loose stock. They recited after the company got started, mornings, and the stock moving.

Nothing happened outside the ordinary routine of the emigrants daily experience, until the company reached Council Bluffs. There were hundreds of emigrants waiting to cross the Missouri River and each one had to wait their turn to cross. Men with big oars pulled the flat boat across the river with two wagons at a time. The men swam the stock across the river. The trail lay over a rolling grassy plain, so the stock had lots of good grass to feed on while the men were getting the wagons and families across on the flat boats. It was the good fortune of this company to have their turn on the flat boat about the middle of the afternoon so they drove on a few miles more from the river up a steep bluff, near what is now the present sight [sic] of Omaha.

They almost had trouble with the Indians a few nights after crossing the Missouri River. Quite a few Indians and squaws rode up and offered to trade buffalo robes for tobacco, beads, and guns. While this trading was going on, a young Indian slipped around to the end of the freight wagon, and was trying to steal some of the arsenal of the company. A thoroughly trained watch dog jumped up on the Indian and his companions drew their bows and were about to let an arrow fly at the dog, but the emigrants saved the life of the dog and soon the Indians left. After crossing the Missouri River they were in the Indian Territory and had to stand guard each night to prevent the stock from being stampeded or stolen by Indians.

The men on horseback would ride ahead of the wagons to find a camping place for the night. They must have good water and grass for the stock and wood for fires if possible. The government men at the post had told the horseback riders always to be in sight of the company, as safety lay only in mutual support. Now they must drive all wagons into a "circle" at night and have all campfires in the center. It was, after a fashion, a fort, and made possible shooting through the cracks of wagons if attacked by Indians. Each family had a fire for their own cooking. If wood for fire was not obtainable, they used twisted grass and buffalo chips.

After the stock had quit feeding on the grass, the men would drive them into this stockade made by the wagons. It would have been disastrous for the emigrants to have lost their oxen or other stock out on the plains so far from their destination.

At this time the company consisted of about one hundred wagons, with quite a large herd of loose stock, cows, horses, and extra oxen, so as to have a change of oxen when advisable.

After crossing the Missouri river there was not a foot of ground surveyed for over a thousand miles. All Indian country clear to Oregon. The Great Plains lay before them, Indians, beasts, prairies, mountains, streams to cross, unfordable rivers, on which they used wagon boxes caulked and tarred for the purpose, and mountains almost impossible to pass over. These were foes they must conquer.

This company of emigrants consisted of a minister, doctors, lawyers, school teachers, millwrights, carpenters, blacksmiths, shoemakers, saddlemakers, harnessmakers, farmers, and stockmen.

The men on horseback drove the stock on ahead of the wagons to find a good place to camp the next night. The loose stock grazed as the train rolled along, but the oxen must wait until time for camping. The success of the trip had to depend on the teams, and stock had to depend on living off the country. When they found a good place to camp for the night they followed their method of camping by driving the wagons so as to form a circle or an oval, the lead wagon falling back to the rear, thus giving each wagon a turn at the lead, the dust arising from the wagon train made this necessary and fair.

The oxen were first unhitched and watered and cared for by some of the men, then other men whose job it was, greased the wagon wheels and looked over each wagon to see that it was in good order for the next day's travel, the boys' task was to milk the cows so the children could have milk for supper. Fires were lighted and the women busied themselves getting supper for the hungry men. The small children were first fed and put to bed in the covered wagons.

There was but little variety in food, mostly it was meat of some kind, biscuits, coffee, beans, dried apple or other kinds of dried fruit. Sometimes they found wild onions or watercress for variety. The men killed a buffalo once in a while, and had buffalo steak for supper, at which time the women would fry a quantity of steak for the next day at noon.

It was late when the men were ready for supper. After all the men had been fed for the night, the grown people gathered around the fire for a while to talk, and sing gospel songs and ask God's care and guidance throughout the night. Then the bugle call, and all turned in for the much needed night's rest. The camp guards divided forces; some slept near the wagons with rifles, others by the stock to be sure they were not stampeded or that the company did not encounter a night attack by the Indians. Very soon the howl of some distant animal or the sound of the oxen chewing their cuds was the only sound.

The camp was up at the first call of the meadowlark. A hasty breakfast of bacon, hot biscuits and strong coffee was made while the men were busy getting the oxen hitched to the wagons. Extra food was cooked for the noon meal as they did not stop long enough at noon to do any cooking, just make some coffee, each minute was precious. When the train company got into the swing of the thing, there was little change from day to day. It was up at the first crack of dawn and through the day the wheels turning on ever toward the setting sun.

Keep moving was the command of the Government Scouts. The problem of health was difficult to settle for the company must keep well. They had little variety in food. Meat was the principal item, the men could get fresh meat most of the time, then they were well supplied with beans, cheese, tea and coffee, and dried fruit. Mother made such good salt rising bread. She would start this yeast in the morning and have it in the wagon with her so she could add more flour when she wanted to knead it into dough so she could have it ready to bake at the campfire. She said this bread was so good to have with cold meat and cheese at the noon meal. She had a Dutch oven of iron with a bale. The oven stood on four legs, and had a big iron lid with a rim turning up to keep the hot coals from falling off. The oven was heated by setting it in front of the campfire on a bed of hot coals, and coals put on top of the lid. The women would make biscuits each morning if they had fuel for the fires. Mother would make them out of a sourdough mixture so they must have a supply of soda and cream of tartar. The biscuits she baked in the Dutch oven and the reflector and a sheet iron stove. They had a good sized tent and when it was storming they would cook and eat in the tent. Mother slept in her wagon and had some of her nieces with her at night. She would unroll her feather bed and make her bed on the packed boxes.

Mother would slice this salt-rising bread and make a jam of dried pears and currants and spread this on the slices of bread. They could not have eggs so the dessert had to be simple. Sometimes she would make a rich biscuit dough and spread fruit of some kind on it, something like we make a jelly cake. She was famous for her fried, dried peach or dried apple pies. Once in a while we at home would prevail on her to make the fried apple or peach pies. She thought this kind of dessert was much better for the men up early and working hard on the plains than the children in her home. This kind of cooking for the noon meal she would do while the men were eating breakfast. Anything left from breakfast was fixed for a snack for the children.

The children enjoyed watching the chattering prairie dogs; they seemed to live in villages of mounds. Occasionally one would hear the song of the meadowlark as it lifted its yellow breast from the grass along the way, or maybe a robin, then a friendly call from a chickadee. It was a source of delight to the children to see how nature protected her creatures; the owl, and the sage hen are the same color as their surroundings.

By advice a long rope had been brought for each wagon in the company for fording streams. The plan was to bunch a number of wagons with teams close together, run a rope and fasten it to the axle tree of each wagon, then men swam across the river with the free end of the rope. Trees had been felled for the logs which were lashed to the side of the wagons to steady them. The swift current of the stream which was shallow and wide drifted the wagons so that mutual support was necessary to cross. Some of the wagons were partly turned over, [but] at last the wagons of the first division were safely across.

The Platte River was a broad shallow stream with sand bars and quicksand. They camped near the river a few days before they could get the other wagons across that belonged to their company. This camp was almost in the midst of a camp of Sioux Indians and they would come to the emigrants' camp, pat their chest and say, "Me good Indian." Mother said they seemed to be different from the other Indians she saw on the plains, tall, straight and manly looking and very anxious to make trades. Some of the men bought ponies from them. She used to tell us about Chimney Rock on the North Platte. Standing alone in the clear atmosphere it did not look far away. But the scout said it would take all day hard riding to get there, so none of their company made the trip. They had to depend largely for stock food on prairie grass, and for their food supply they must hunt deer,

*Belle seated in chair with her children (left to right) Lora, Opal, Allen, and Ida.*

buffalo and other wild meats. So many people were to travel along the same route that there was a wild scramble to get started early each morning for they must camp early in the evening. The oxen were slow in the morning and hard to goad on the way, but as camping time approached seeming to sense that soon they would be watered and fed, they hurried on. The train had to get in the habit of camping early so the stock would have more time to feed on the grass. They drove along cows to milk, and steers for beef, but wild game was plentiful along the trail and the hunters kept the company well supplied with meat, but the emigrants were anxious to trade or buy sugar, flour, bacon, beans, tea and coffee. Whenever they could purchase these things they did so.

A dry camp for tonight, the cattle had to content themselves with the juice from the grass. The men would gather all the wood they could find along the way each day. They had no serious trouble with the Indians, but quite a few sudden alarms, maybe the Indians would take a fancy for the shirt some man had on and would want to trade for the shirt. They would offer to trade buffalo robes for guns, tobacco, or beads. The emigrants would not trade or sell a gun to the Indians.

One day they met a few emigrants who had gone on ahead of the rest of their company, something the guides told them not to do. They had turned around and were driving back as fast as they could. About one hundred Indians had attacked them and were circling them on ponies and firing at them. The Indians left as soon as the men on horse-back started out to chase them. Their object in riding in circles was to prevent anyone getting a better target by their riding straight away. In 1852 the cholera was very bad on the plains, [but] in this company they were very fortunate in not having very much sickness. At one time on the trip they came to a place where they intended to camp. There they found a man dead with a blanket wrapped over his body. The train captains sent the ox teams on and the men buried the man. They did not know the cause of the death. That night was late when they camped at a dry camp, but there was good grass for the stock.

One day a government scout came up to them and told them to double guard that night as the Indians had attacked a small train of emigrants the night before and had killed some of them, drove off the stock, cut open feather beds and scattered other things over the camping place. Our family's company was large, and well armed, and guarded each night. Their train had increased to over one hundred wagons with lots of stock, and a good number of young men to care for the stock. The men were all well armed and good shots.

## The Eastern Slope of the Rockies

The emigrants would rest on Sundays, unless conditions were very unfavorable, then they would travel. Most of the emigrants thought man and beast should have one day for rest. As the eastern slope of the mountains approached and the teams drew their loads ever higher and higher, it became evident that they must double up on teams five or six yoke of oxen on each wagon. The clear dry atmosphere and out-of-door life agreed with the emigrants. There was nothing dull about the days spent climbing toward the top of the Rocky Mountains. One day a whirlwind tore canvas sheets from some of the wagons, then nearby thunder and lightening made the mountains tremble. The women and larger chil-dren had to walk most of the way, by the side of their wagons, while the oxen plodded slowly and steadily along.

Arriving at South Pass in the Rockies they drank out of the first streams of water flowing west to the Pacific Ocean. They followed its way until it entered the Snake River, and then the Columbia, to the Pacific Ocean. Down the western slope of the Rockies the train turned their teams. I am sure each man and woman breathed a silent prayer to God, that the hard work was over. After coming down the mountain, they came to the Great Desert. Fifty miles of dry plains without any water, the emigrants had filled all water barrels and jugs with water to take with them. They drove all night and late into the next day. Night driving was not too bad but the next day was hard on man and beast. When they reached Green River the men stopped and unyoked the oxen and let them go down to the river to drink. Green River was a large and beautiful stream, with considerable timber and quaking-asp. The train layed by to rest the teams and stock. The women washed and did extra cooking. The men looked over all parts of the wagons and greased the wagon wheels, for a breakdown on the road would tie up the whole company. Dusty roads, the dust so fine and dry at times that one could hardly see the tongue yoke of oxen.

Fort Hall lay in the territory now comprising Idaho. The Snake River is said to be the most remarkable river because it is no wider where it joins the Columbia River than at its source.

Two of the most wonderful sights on the Snake River are Shoshone Falls and Twin Falls. At the Fort they obtained another supply of necessary things. Slowly they traveled by easy stages. It was hot, dry and dusty. They had but little sickness in their train. One night they were in a terrible thunder storm. It was accompanied by lightening. It seemed the heavens were on fire and the peals of thunder made the earth fairly tremble. One man in the company died on Burnt River from summer complaint. The men took some lumber from the wagon boxes and made a coffin, lined it with homespun sheeting and buried him as nice as was possible out on the plains. Crossing the Blue Mountains gave them but little idea of what was before them. The journey was becoming tedious to them day by day. Watch and guard duties every night were wearing on the menfolk. The ox teams were getting sore footed and poor and they were still far from the Willamette Valley, their goal. Through the Umatilla, John Day, and the Deschutes, fording and floundering with their big ox wagons towards the end of the trail. Moving on steadily always in order to get through the mountains before the grass was gone.

Pathetically they were often compelled to leave faithful beasts in the wilderness to starve, but there was no help for it, often the animals were shot to end their misery.

The East side of the Cascade Mountains was a long hard pull for the oxen. The men put on six or eight yoke of oxen on each wagon. It took more time but was much easier on the teams. It had been hard to find pasturage for the stock on the mountain range, so the wagon train camped early in the afternoon, so that the oxen and other stock would have more time to feed and rest. By this time the stock were getting quite thin and worn from the long trip. After they crossed the backbone of the mountain they had to go down Laurel Hill on the Barlow Road. Mother said it was by far the worst hill they had on the entire trip. The men had to cut trees down to fasten on the back of the wagons with the branches on, to act as brake to let the wagons down the hill. When they finally got the whole company down, they camped in a nice valley with good grass for the stock. They rested a few days then started on for Portland. Before they got to Portland some men came to meet the train with supplies to sell. To get a doctor to locate in their community, or a teacher to teach that winter. Some man from Yamhill County, Oregon Territory, wanted my mother to teach his children and maybe a few neighbor children in his home. She accepted and spent the winter of 1852 in Yamhill County.

Father crossed the plains in 1851 and the most impressive thing to him was Laurel Hill. He said he wanted to see if in later life it looked as steep. So years after he went back over that part of the old emigrant road. He said it was just as steep and impressive as in 1851 and he was sure only the pioneers would have tried it. The marks of the chains and ropes were still on the old logs at the bottom of the hill. When her school was out in the spring of 1853 mother went on up to Polk County to Monmouth. On September 27, 1853, she was married to Ezekiel Allen Shirley, who had crossed the plains from Kentucky in 1851 with his sister Elizabeth and her husband, T. Davidson, who settled on his donation claim of 640 acres near Buena Vista.

Father filed on his donation claim in Polk County as he was not married at that time, he was entitled to only 320 acres of land. He built quite a large log house with a big fireplace in one end. He did his cooking on the fireplace and on a sheetiron stove that he had used on the plains. He had a team of oxen that he did his plowing with, and got out timbers for his barn. The timbers were all twelve inches square, hand hewn and put together with oak pegs. Harvest tools were scythe, cradle, rake, and pitchfork. Father and mother lived on the donation place for about twenty-five years. Father had a house in Monmouth where they lived in the winter, so the children could go to school. Their children were raised on the old donation farm. Father built a very good house on the farm and used the log house for a woodshed. One night about Christmas time the house burned. I think this was in 1868. Then we lived most of the time in Monmouth. I think it was about 1869 father built another good house on the farm.

Father brought appleseeds across the plains with him, which he planted. Then he grafted or budded other fruit on these seedling apple trees until years after he had a very good variety of fruit. In the farm home the family lived all summer, when winter came we moved back to the house in Monmouth for the school year. About this time father was thinking of getting his boys on government land in the northeastern part of Washington Territory.

## Washington Territory

In the summer of 1879 my father had been hearing such wonderful reports of the stock and grain farms in the rolling hills of the Palouse country of Washington Territory. Father had four boys, and three of them old enough to file on government land for a homestead. So he left a man and wife to care for the farm and stock during his absence. In September of 1879 he began to make preparations to go to Waitsburg, Walla Walla County,

Washington Territory for one or two years to look over the country and see if he could get his boys settled on government land. In October of that year he shipped by steamboat down the Willamette River from Salem to Portland, Oregon. The next day we started by boat from Portland up the Columbia River to The Dalles at Celilo Falls. A narrow gauge railroad had been built to take the place of the old portage mule train around the falls. Then back on the upper Columbia River on a steam turning paddle wheel boat on our way to Wallula landing. Father had shipped a team of horses and carriage to Wallula. This landing seemed a desolate place and our destination by water. Father and the boys drove the team from Wallula to Walla Walla, about thirty miles, I think. When father put mother and grandmother and me on the train he told mother which hotel to go to when we got to Walla Walla. Grandmother, mother and I went on Dr. Baker's narrow gauge railroad. We did not have to ride on the old passenger car. This was a new coach. We saw the old passenger car with the seats along the side. On that trip I saw my first flock of prairie chickens. They were beautiful birds. There was a great flock of them. I saw my first coyote, the train stopped and a few of the men got off the train and shot at the coyote, it ran off through the bunch grass, looking back at them.

Our train continued and when we finally arrived in Walla Walla father and the boys were at the depot waiting for us. He took us to our hotel for the night, and the next day we drove to Waitsburg, Washington Territory, a little town in Walla Walla County. That was to be our home for the next year. My brother and I went to school that year in Waitsburg. In January of 1880 my grandmother Roundtree fell and broke her hip and leg. On February 11, 1880, she died. She crossed the plains in 1853 with her husband and youngest son, she was 88 years old. Grandfather Roundtree had settled in Lewis County in 1853.

I am going to tell you about an incident that happened over sixty years ago and it made a lasting impression on me at the time, even today it is an event that I remember very well. After we went to Waitsburg, we used to make weekend trips looking over the country. We spent the night at a place where a Twenty Mule freight wagon and team had camped for the night. The wagon was large with high box loaded with some kind of freight. Then another wagon chained or fixed fast in some way to the lead wagon as a trailer and loaded with freight, as I remember the freight was consigned to some miners. Father had us up early the next morning to see the teamster hitch up the mules to the wagon. When the teamster had unhitched the night before the harness had been left on the ground in the mules' place. When he started to hitch his team to the wagon he did a lot of talking to them, then one mule after the other would come around to their proper places. I thought the mules knew as much about the job as the teamster did. When they were all in their places, at the command from the teamster the lead team would lean forward in their collars and then the next span of mules would lean forward and straighten out, so down to the

237

wheel mules. The driver of the team drives with a jerk line and rides one of the wheel mules on the left hand side, then the twenty mule team was rolling on it's journey. I don't remember that they even had the twenty mules but that seemed to be the name given this freight team.

On one of these weekend trips we saw one of these big thorough brace stage coaches drawn by four and six horses, the stage had no springs, the body swung on heavy straps as the vehicle jolted along in and out of the ruts in the road and at each pitch of the vehicle the passengers would slide until they came to the end of the seat, or hit another passenger, all horses going as fast as they could and the stage in a cloud of dust.

After school closed in June of 1880, father started with his family for Spokane Falls, as it was then called. From Waitsburg to Snake River was mostly a stock country. The hills were covered with a luxuriant growth of bunch grass. The grass grew in such large bunches that stock on the range were very fat. Father said this bunch grass was like cured hay for the stock. The large ranges were taken up by homesteaders. Little one room box houses of boards, the cracks battened, were scattered here and there through the hills and valleys. We crossed the Snake River at the Almota Ferry, and stayed with Mr. and Mrs. Spalding for a few days. We found out that a day or so before, a cloudburst in the Almota Canyon had washed out the road up the canyon, so our journey was postponed until they could make the road passable for teams. Father and mother were so glad to become acquainted with Mr. and Mrs. Spalding, forming a friendship that lasted through life. We finally started for Colfax and spent a few days with father's sister and other relatives. Then on to Rosalia and spent some time with friends and former neighbors there, father looking for land. Shortly we went to Spokane Falls. At that time there were no bridges across the river nearer than Cowlys bridge, twelve or fifteen miles above Spokane. The falls were magnificent when the wind blew the spray from one side of the river to the other. The spray would make quite a green spot of grass where it would fall. So much more water went over the falls then, than at the present time. When father started back he wanted to go by way of Farmington to look at some land, then to see some old friends and former neighbors living at Palouse City, and Moscow, Idaho.

In some way he met a man who had proved up on his preemption claim in Whitman County and was anxious to sell. Father drove down to the place, looked it over and bought the 160 acres. This farm was near the present town of Johnson, and was our home for many years. Sixty years in Whitman County.

There were no schools in the district when father first settled on this farm. Later a school house was built. Church and Sunday school and community entertainments were held in the school house. Mrs. Miles Hooper was the first teacher, she had all grades. Fletcher Staley and I were the only ones taking high school work. The young men of the neighborhood bought an organ for church and Sunday school. A. J. Green kept the organ in his home and took it to the school house each Sunday. When the weather was nice we would have a neighborhood picnic dinner, then later we would have a lot of fun singing and visiting together. There was no rivalry nor envy. Everybody knew everybody even if they had not met before. The pioneers' doors were never locked. What was of interest to one was of equal interest to all. Sorrow in one family became sorrow for all. I think it was in the year of 1881 father had a good house built on this farm, the boys were on farms of their own. He and mother thought they would sell the old donation farm in Oregon. He had the family piano and house hold goods shipped to Almota. The boys took the wagon and teams down to the river and brought the piano and other freight. I remember how happy I was when we had the piano and our furniture in our new home. Father and mother both could sing very well and both could read music, and one brother taught both voice and piano. It was the custom for the neighbors on Sunday afternoons that winter to gather at father's home around the piano and sing until they all had to go home and care for the stock.

Father's home was a haven for preachers. Both he and mother were deeply interested in the religious life of the community. One cold winter day the wind was blowing and snow drifting, I looked out our front window and saw a man coming into our yard. He had left his horse at the gate, with bridle reins thrown over the gate post. He was so cold he could hardly walk as he came to the house. I went to the door to meet him and he was so nearly frozen he could hardly speak. But he told me his name was Cushing Eels, [and] that was enough, [for] everyone knew and loved the Reverend Cushing Eels. I started to fix the fire. He said would I please get a basin of snow for him, which I did and helped him get his gloves or mittens off his hands into the basin of snow. By the time father and mother came home he was quite comfortable. Father had met him some place and was very glad to have him in our home. Just think, I had rubbed snow on the ears of the Reverend Cushing Eels, the founder of Whitman College. The Reverend Eels told us about a small printing press which had been brought from the Sandwich Islands and set up at Lapwai. Books were printed in the Nez Perce language by the Reverend Spalding. This was the first printing press in the northwest.

## On Wild Horse Butte

My brother and I used to ride horseback over Wild Horse Butte, and from the top of the Butte looking over the hills and valleys was a beautiful sight. Hills and valleys covered with a luxuriant growth of bunch grass that rolled in billows with the breeze like the waves of the ocean. This beautiful bunch grass was knee high to the stock, and range horses and cattle were rolling fat. The ranch men would cut this grass for winter feed for cattle.

The range horses could live out on the range all winter on this grass. The horses would paw the snow off the grass with their forefoot or hoof. The plowing of this bunch grass was quite a job. The grass roots were tough and not easily broken. Besides, there were so many sunflower roots which were very tough. They looked something like a sugar beet root. When the plow struck one of these roots it was sure to jerk the plow out of the ground or give the ploughman a good jerk. When the roots were dry they were an excellent substitute for stove wood. Mother liked to have them when she had bread to bake or meat to roast. My brothers didn't like to get them from the sod. When harrowing the ground the harrow would pull them out of the ground and then they would be thrown in a pile to dry. When the roots were partly dry they were loaded into the wagon and taken to the woodpile so they could finish drying for summer wood. It would take two days for the men to haul a load of wood from the nearest place in the mountains, where they could buy wood, so fuel was very scarce and the sunflower roots were a good substitute for summer wood, for just the labor.

# THE AUTHOR

Naomi Stanley Kulp was born and spent her early childhood in Enterprise in the Wallowa Mountains of northeastern Oregon. When she was three, her family moved to her grandfather's ranch in the Touchet Valley. She enjoyed growing up in the valley until she attended Oregon State University and obtained her Home Economics Education degree.

A creative cook, she enjoys traveling and collecting recipes from interesting restaurants around the world. She has many interests, including grandchildren and gardening. A talented floral designer and skilled photographer, her award-winning designs have been published and she holds copyrights on her sculptures for floral designs.

Researching family history and genealogy holds special interest for Naomi and she encourages relatives to participate and to share and publish family documents. Annual McCaw family reunions in Washington and Oregon provide opportunities for information and recipe exchange.

Naomi is a member of the Oregon-California Trails Association and Northwest Historical Societies. She plans to travel the Oregon Trail in 1996, retracing the route followed by her great grandparents, William and Sarah McCaw.


# THE ARTISTS

Linda Newberry is a native Californian who lived nine years on the north Oregon coast before moving to Port Townsend, Washington. She has twenty years experience as a naturalist and environmental educator. Presently she works for the Jamestown S'Klallam Tribe. Linda created the pen and ink drawings of birds native to the Touchet Valley.

Evelyn Hicks is a freelance artist in Portland, Oregon. Her illustrations have appeared in several publications, including those of the Oregon Historical Society Press and Oregon Council for the Humanities, and have won publishing awards for the Audubon Society of Portland. Evelyn created the pencil drawings seen in this book.

# REFERENCES

*All About Home Baking*, General Foods Corporation, 1933.

Findley, Caroline, "A Sketch of Pioneer Days, 1847," Transactions of The Oregon Pioneer Association, 1926, pp. 23-29, courtesy of Sieglinde Smith, Librarian, Research Library, Oregon Historical Society, Portland, Oregon.

Gilbert, Frank T., Historic *Sketches of Walla Walla, Whitman, Columbia, and Garfield Counties in Washington Territory*, Portland, Oregon, 1882.

*Ladies of the Presbyterian Church Cookbook*, Prescott, Washington, 1903.

Laidlaw, Ellis and Elvira, "Wait's Mill," excerpt from an article by Vance Orchard, *Waitsburg Times*, Waitsburg, Washington, 1993.

Letters of Samuel Erwin, *Waitsburg Times*, Waitsburg, Washington.

McCaw, Robert H., *Two Hundred and Fifty Years of McCaws*, 1984.

Orchard, Vance, *Walla Walla Story*, 1988 Washington Centennial Edition of 1953 publication.

Osborn, Josiah, "Letter from Oregon, April 7, 1848," published in Oquawka *Spectator*, Henderson County, Illinois, 1848, courtesy of Lawrence Dodd, Archivist, Penrose Library, Whitman College, Walla Walla, Washington.

*The Heritage Newsletter*, Albany, Oregon, September, 1993.

"This Was Harvesting," voice recording, Penrose Library, Whitman College, Walla Walla, Washington, courtesy of Lawrence L. Dodd and Lawrence Paynter.

Whitman, Narcissa, "Narcissa Prentiss Whitman Diary, 11 August 1836," in: Marcus and Narcissa Whitman Papers (BANC MSS P-A 341), courtesy of B. Hardwick, Ph.D., Head, Manuscripts Division, The Bancroft Library, University of California, Berkeley.

Recipe References:

Divinity Meringue for Lemon Pie, *Eating Well* magazine, February, 1994

Grandfather's Candy Shop Caramels, Jo Asbury

# RECIPE INDEX

Please send Wagon Wheels *&* Wild Roses Cookbook to:

Name _____

Address _____

City _____

State/Zip _____

Telephone No. ( ) _____

| Price | Quantity | Total |
|---|---|---|
| $22.95 | _____ | $ _____ |
| Shipping *&* handling $3.00 per book | | $ _____ |
| Washington residents add 8.2% sales tax | | $ _____ |
| Total enclosed | | $ _____ |

Send check and order coupon to:

Naomi Stanley Kulp
Wild Rose Press
818 S. Marine Hills Way
Federal Way, WA 98003